DIANA
following in her footsteps

Neville Ness House

DIANA
following in her footsteps

BY

ANTONIO ROSSI

AND

SARAH-JANE BENTLEY

DIANA
following in her footsteps

First published in Great Britain in 2017 by

Neville Ness House Ltd

www.nevillenesshouse.com

A CIP catalogue record for this book is available from the British Library

PB ISBN 978-1999746940
HB ISBN 978-1999746957

Vignettes by Sarah-Jane Bentley

Illustrations by Antonio Rossi

Cover layout by Ebooksbydesign

DIANA
following in her footsteps

About this book . . .

You will be transported into the fascinating world Diana, Princess of Wales, occupied in the British capital, London. *Diana: Following in her footsteps*, takes you to the cathedral where she was married, the palaces where she lived, the abbey where her funeral was conducted and the apartment block she called home until a king-in-waiting came courting. Suitable for every generation, young and old.

You will experience:

- the places where she ate – from the salubrious celebrity haunts to the burger bars where she used to take William and Harry for what she told them was 'a nosh'
- the fashion houses where she shopped for fine clothes;
- the hospitals where she tended to the sick;
- the special places where her memory is preserved

And then there are the places where she let her hair down:

- an outrageously gay venue on the wrong side of the Thames;
- the grand Royal Opera House where she left the Royal Box and her surprised husband to join the dancing on stage; and
- the Mayfair nightclub where she drank at the bar disguised as a policewoman.

You will find it's ALL here . . . and so much more

DIANA
Following in her footsteps
What's inside . . .

1. FLAT 60, COLEHERNE COURT, Old Brompton Road SW5 0EF

2. YOUNG ENGLAND KINDERGARTEN, St Saviours Hall, St George's Square, SW1V 2HP

3. BUCKINGHAM PALACE, SW1 1AA

4. ASPREY & GARARD, 167 New Bond Street, W1S 4AY

5. GOLDSMITHS HALL, Foster Lane, EC2V 6BN

6. ST PAUL'S CATHEDRAL, Ludgate Hill, EC4M 8AD

7. CLARENCE HOUSE, St James's, The Mall, SW1A 1BA

8. ANNABEL'S, Berkeley Square, W1J 5QB

9. ST MARY'S HOSPITAL, Praed Street, W2 1NY

10. WETHERBY SCHOOL, 11 Pembridge Square, W2 4ED

11. KENSINGTON PALACE, W8 4PX

12. SAN LORENZO, 22 Beauchamp Place, SW3 1 NH

13. CLARIDGE'S, Brook Street, W1K 4HR

14. STICKY FINGERS, 1A Phillimore Gardens, W8 7QB

15. ROYAL OPERA HOUSE, Bow Street, WC2E 9DD

16. KASPIA, 18 Bruton Place, W1J 6LY (now Bellamy's)

17. HYDE PARK (to the west of Park Lane)

18. VOGUE HOUSE, Hanover Square, W1S 1JU

19. HARVEY NICHOLS, Knightsbridge, SW1X 7RJ

20. LANESBOROUGH HOTEL, Hyde Park Corner, SW1X 7TA

21. VANDERBILT RACQUET CLUB, 31 Sterne Street, W12 8AB

22. ROYAL VAUXHALL TAVERN, 372 Kennington Lane, SE11 5HY

23. THE HARBOUR CLUB, Watermeadow Lane, SW6

DIANA
Following in her footsteps
What's inside . . .

Flat 60 Coleherne Court, Old Brompton Road, SW5 OEF

This is where it all began. Bought for her by her mother as a coming-of-age present, the apartment was Diana's home when Prince Charles began courting her, but he never visited the block. To avoid being photographed with her, he invariably insisted she drive herself to meet him at a secret rendezvous of his choosing. When the relationship became more serious his manservant Stephen Barry drove her to Highgrove, the Prince's Gloucestershire estate, and returned her to Coleherne Court at daybreak so that it appeared she had spent the night at home. Diana shared the three-bedroom flat with three flatmates, Carolyn Pride (later the talkative singer Carolyn Bartholomew, as it says in the biography, **DIANA: Always There.**), Anne Bolton and Virginia Pitman each paying her £18 for the weekly rental of their rooms. When Diana announced that she was to marry the Heir to the Throne, Carolyn was on a throne herself: 'I was sitting on the loo when Di broke the news through the door. There was a lot of shouting and we all broke into tears. It was very emotional.' The Princess was to say that her times at Coleherne Court were the happiest of her life: 'Away from my father's stately home and my husband's palace, I felt normal in Earl's Court.' Prices of apartments in the block have soared since it became associated with Diana – No. 60 was sold to a Japanese buyer for £100,000 – almost double what Mrs Shand Kydd had paid for it just twenty months earlier.

'For God's sake ring me up, I'm going to need you'

Diana in a note to her flatmates when she moved out of Coleherne Court

COLEHERNE COURT

Young England Kindergarten, St Saviours Hall, St.George's Square, London SW1V 2HP

This Pimlico nursery gave 19-year-old Diana her first job. One of the most established nurseries in the capital, it feeds pupils to top schools including Hill House, which was Prince Charles's primary school, and Wetherby, subsequently attended by both William and Harry. To Charles's consternation the Princess was photographed here in a see-through skirt at the time of her engagement. Right up to the time of her death Diana remained a close friend of the school's principal, Margaret Hodge, and a collection of 13 letters she hand-wrote wrote to Mrs Hodge were expected to fetch £20,000 at auction. One note was dotted with smudges which, Diana said, were Prince William's fingerprints. When referring to herself and her husband in such letters, Diana wrote 'Mr and Mrs Wales', the same form of address adopted by William and Kate today. Margaret Hodge, who was privy to many of Diana's secrets said, 'I know she was very much in love with Prince Charles and just wanted to be loved in return.'

'Hugs can do great amounts of good – especially for children'

Diana

Buckingham Palace, SW1A 1AA

Nowhere else during her short life as a member of the Royal Family did Diana, Princess of Wales, experience both majesty and menace. It was from the Palace Press Office that her engagement to Prince Charles was happily announced in 1981, it was within the palace walls that the couple gave a television interview with Diana declaring her love for her husband (to which he responded: 'Whatever in love means'), and it was on the balcony of the palace's East Wing that Diana sealed her wedding day with a very public kiss. Living with Prince Charles in one of the royal apartments Diana loved mixing with the staff as much as she dreaded inevitable meetings with her husband's courtiers who tried to make her behave as princesses had in days gone by – reverential and always taking second place in the limelight. Chef Darren McGrady recalls, 'If she was on her own for lunch, she'd actually come and eat on the countertop in the kitchen. I'd make a tray for her and I'd just carry on tidying up the kitchen and as we were chatting she would offer to help me with the chores. The rest of the royals would never do that.' The fairy tale seemed to be coming true. All too soon, however, a dark shadow blighted Diana's happiness: it came in the form of the courtiers who made her life a misery when she refused to follow protocol to the letter. Charles had already upset her by pinching her puppy fat suggesting that she needed to lose weight, he was unaware that his bride was sneaking down to McGrady's kitchen late at night to make herself a sandwich or enjoy a tub of ice cream – comfort food.

'It was as if Charles was married to them, not me; they are so patronising, it drives me mad'

Diana on certain Palace courtiers

4

Asprey & Garrard, 167 New Bond Street, W1S 4AY

Are you torn between buying an engagement ring from a magnificent store like the Asprey & Garrard one in Mayfair you can colour in here, OR picking one out of a catalogue? Well you can do both – The Princess viewed those on sale in the store before picking out one in a brochure she noticed on the shop's counter . . . and the catalogue won. The ring she selected (which now adorns the finger of a woman born to be her daughter-in-law, Kate Middleton) – consists of a large oval 12 karat Ceylon sapphire surrounded by a cluster of 14 diamonds set in 18 karat white gold.   Diana's association with the store – now the property of the U.S. clothing group Tommy Hilfiger - does not end with the baubles she acquired from it: her close friend Rosa Monckton was Chief Executive of Asprey & Garrard (which are once again two separate stores, with Garrard conducting its business in Albemarle Street). The two women frequently holidayed together and when Ms Monckton lost a baby she was expecting, Diana offered her close friend a plot in her Kensington Palace garden for the infant's last resting place.

> 'Do you want to feel my engagement ring? I'd better not lose it before the big day or they won't know who I am.'
> Diana to a blind woman at a Palace Garden Party

Goldsmiths Hall, Foster Lane, EC2V 6BN

This is the scene of Diana's first official engagement with her fiancé. She had hitherto dressed conservatively but this night the world saw a dramatic change of image when she arrived in a low-cut décolleté black taffeta dress. 'Di's daring debut' read newspaper headlines the following day. Diana let it be known that she was mortified. This was her first real experience in the glare of the cameras as a royal-to-be. Her first experience, too, of how minutely the Press would be observing her every movement and just how merciless the media could be. 'Wasn't that a mighty feast to set before a King,' the aristocratic octogenarian Lady Diana Cooper quipped when she saw the photographs of Diana in her daring frock.

'When virtue and modesty enlighten her charms, the lustre
of a beautiful woman is brighter than the stars of heaven,
and the influence of her power it is in vain to resist.'
Akhenaton

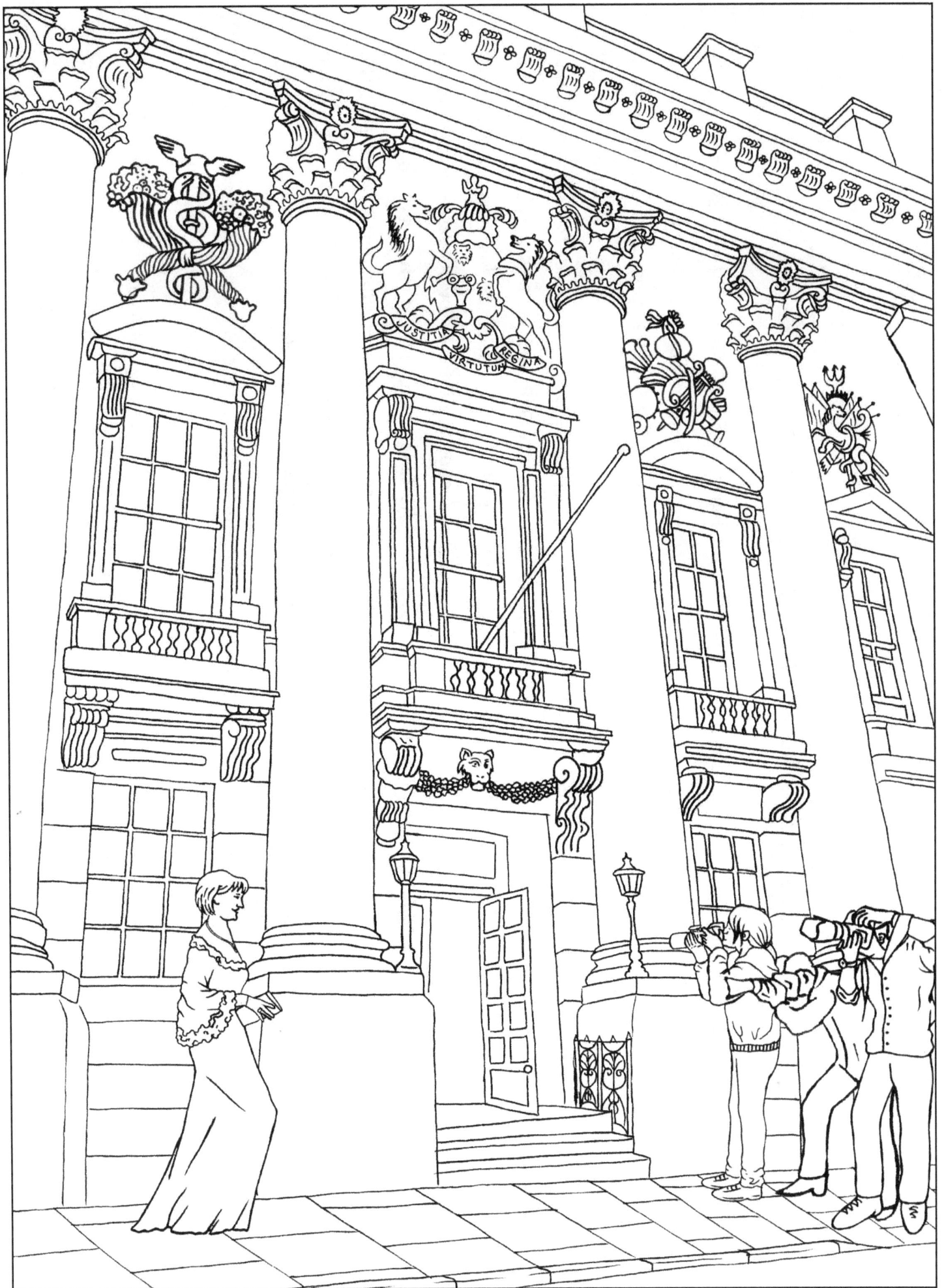

St Paul's Cathedral, Ludgate Hill, EC4M 8AD

IIt was described as 'the wedding of the century' when Prince Charles made Diana his Princess at St Paul's Cathedral on 29 July, 1981. The ceremony was watched by an estimated global audience of 750 million. Although Charles had known her for several years it was not until the summer of 1980 that he took a serious interest in her when both were guests at a country house party. He invited her to Cowes for a sailing holiday aboard the Royal Yacht Britannia. Next, she was invited to Balmoral Castle, the Windsors' Scottish home, to meet his family. They had been seeing each other for six months before he proposed to her on February 3, 1981 in the nursery at Windsor Castle. Their engagement became official on February 24 after Diana had selected her elegant £28,000 engagement ring. 3,500 guests attended the wedding – Charles had chosen St Paul's over Westminster Abbey because it could hold more people and provided a longer route for the tens of thousands who were to line it. As Lady Diana for the last time, the most watched public beauty since Jackie Onassis arrived exactly on time at the Cathedral in a glass coach. The Cathedral sits on Ludgate Hill, the highest point in the city of London. It can be reached by tube at St Paul's Station, by the nearby City Thameslink station, or by bus.

'Neither of us will ever forget the atmosphere. It was electric, almost unbelievable'

– Prince Charles on their wedding day

'Enjoy something like that? It was terrifying. Such a long walk up the aisle for a start'

– Diana on the wedding

Clarence House, St James's, The Mall SW1A 1BA

This was Diana's home from the day her engagement was announced up until her wedding day. It had also been the home of Queen Elizabeth, the Queen Mother, from 1953 until her death in 2002. Two days before their wedding Diana threatened to call the whole thing off after discovering that Charles was still seeing Mrs Parker Bowles (who has since become the Duchess of Cornwall). She later revealed 'I went upstairs, had lunch with my sisters and said "I can't marry him, I can't do this," They were wonderful and one of them said "Well bad luck, Duch, your face is on the tea towels so you're too late to chicken out".' After the Prince assured her that his affair was over, Diana agreed to go through with the service. On the eve of the wedding she even slipped out of Clarence House to mingle with crowds gathering on The Mall. On the day itself (according to one of the bridesmaids) she wandered around singing the TV ad theme Just One Cornetto to calm her nerves. Later, a million people cheered the newly married couple as they returned from St Paul's in the open-topped State landau. Today Clarence House – which is open to the public during summer months – is now the official London residence of Charles and Camilla. Standing beside St James's Palace, the House was built between 1825 and 1827 to the designs of John Nash for Prince William Henry, the-then Duke of Clarence. He lived there as King William IV from 1830 until 1837. It was also the home of the Princess Elizabeth and her husband following their marriage in 1947.

'I have the best mother-in-law in the world' –

Diana on the Queen

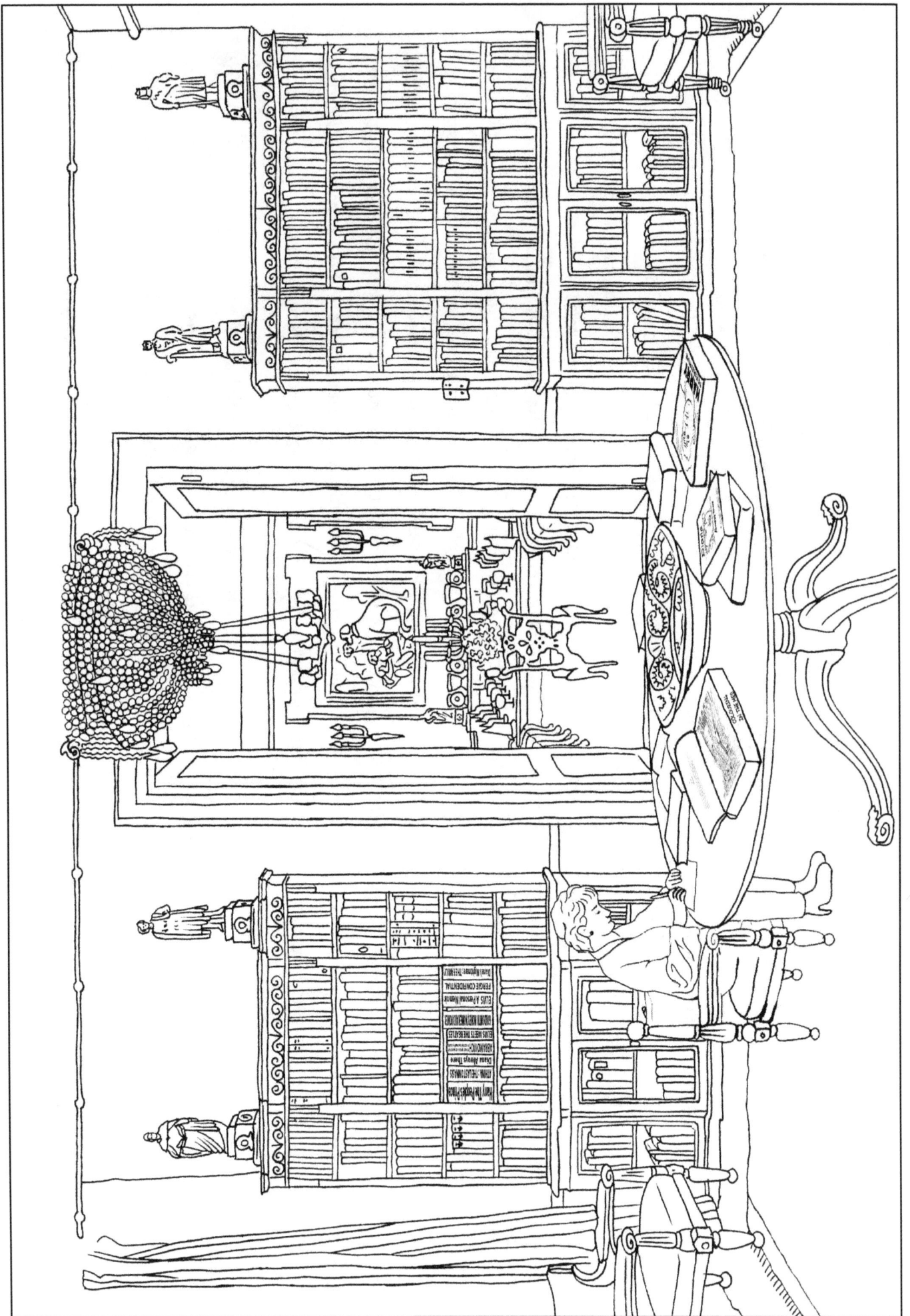

Annabel's, Berkeley Square, W1J 5QB

The club is named after Diana's friend and mother figure, Lady Annabel Goldsmith. Dressed as policewomen, Diana and her about-to-become sister-in-law, Sarah Ferguson, turned up at the club on the eve of Sarah's wedding to Prince Andrew, having failed to gatecrash his stag party at Holland Park where, in uniform, they had planned to 'arrest' him. The giggling pair aroused the suspicions of Annabel's members who were surprised to see 'policewomen' drinking Bucks Fizz at the bar. Diana later complained: 'The wig was hot and uncomfortable and my feet were killing me – the shoes were two sizes too small. But you have to have a laugh sometimes.' Diana and Fergie were by no means the only ones to have shocked there: Frank Sinatra had a fling with a hat check girl, John Wayne got hopelessly drunk at the bar and a living princess, who shall remain nameless, once revealed all on the dance floor. Diana, however, was to say that the club held bad memories for her. She knew full well that this was the venue where Prince Charles danced with Camilla for the very first time – by no means the first or the last of love matches made in what has been described as Britain's most exclusive and yet naughtiest club.

'Diana's repartee became an essential part of the Sunday lunches at my home in Ham, interrupted occasionally when she vanished to the kitchen to do the washing up. There was no protocol. I think she did regard me as something of a surrogate mother.'

Lady Annabel Goldsmith

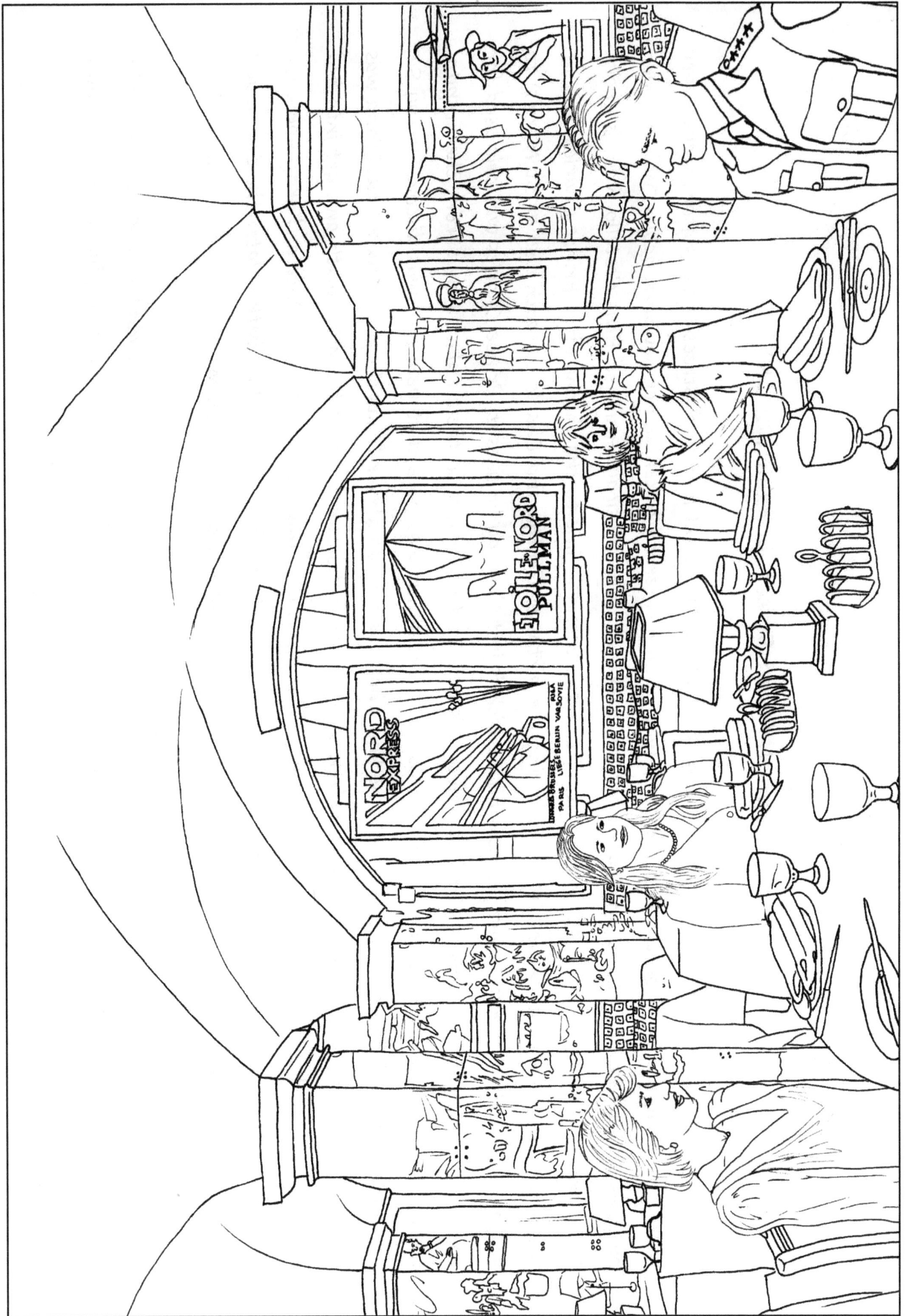

St Mary's Hospital, Praed Street, London W2 1NY.

The steps leading down from the Lindo Wing of St Mary's Hospital in Praed Street, Paddington, were never more photographed than on the two occasions when Diana emerged clutching her newborn babies, William born on June 21, 1982 and Harry on September 15, 1984 (for the musically-minded Elvis Costello was also born there and Billy Fury died there). William is, of course, second in line to the throne after Prince Charles, and at the time of his birth Harry was third. Following the births of George and Charlotte (both also at St Mary's) to William and Kate, however, Harry is now fifth which is just the way he likes it. Prince Charles was criticised for going off to play polo as soon as he had driven his wife and sons back to their Palace home from the hospital where, to be fair, he had attended both births. Incidentally, it was here that penicillin was discovered (by Sir Alexander Fleming) as well as heroin. All who knew her say that whatever faults she might have had, Diana was a perfect mother. 'I want to bring my children up with perfect security. I hug them to death and get into bed with them at night. I always feed them love and affection, it is so important,' she said. Once a charity home for the 'deserving poor', St Mary's acquired a strong royal connection when Princess Elizabeth – later the Queen and then the Queen Mother – became its patron after which it became popular with members of society, politicians, entertainers and, of course, other royals.

'Diana always loved babies' –
her father, the late Earl Spencer

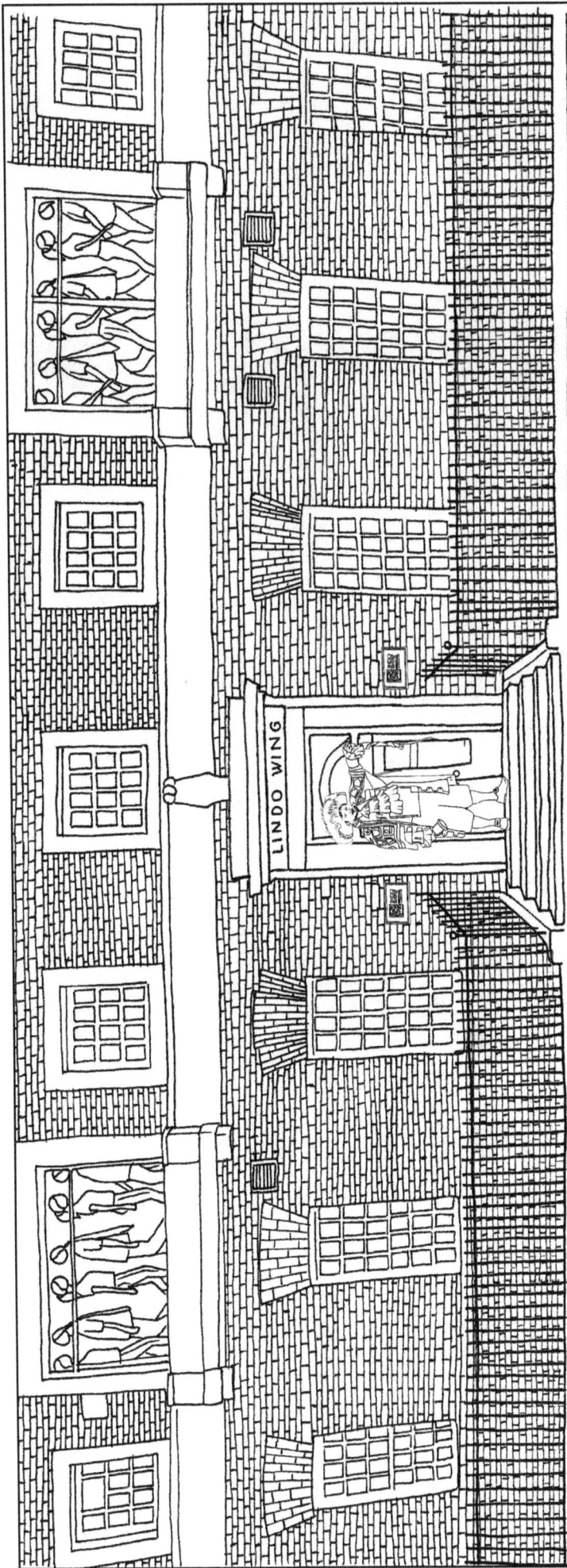

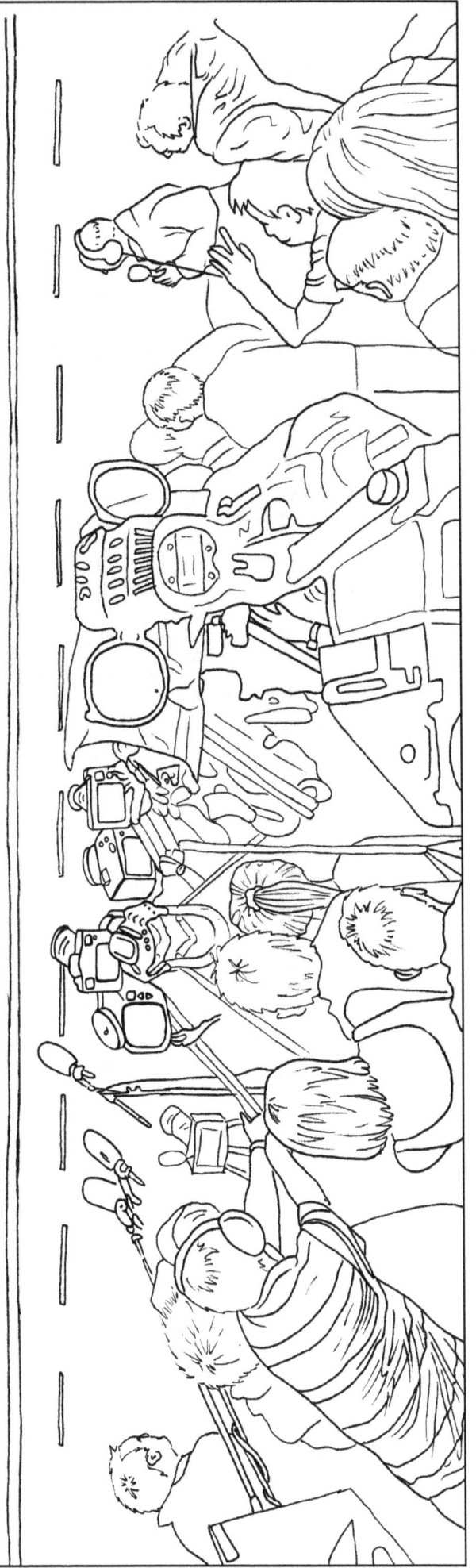

LINDO WING

Wetherby School, 11 Pembridge Square, W2 4ED

Diana made history when she took her youngest son to Wetherby on January 15, 1987 making William, then aged four, the first member of the Royal Family to attend a public school with boys just like himself. Like Prince Charles, other senior royals had begun their education in private rooms at Buckingham Palace. Other Wetherby parents remember Diana regularly delivering William, and later Harry, to the school on mornings when official engagements permitted. Although she was always accompanied by a royal protection officer, the Princess would drive the boys the short distance from Kensington Palace to the double-fronted building where the schoolrooms are spread over five floors overlooking the attractive Pembroke Square Gardens. Just like all the other pupils, the princes were required to wear the regular school uniform – grey shorts, white shirts, red tie, grey peaked cap and a matching blazer emblazoned with the school's WS logo. Diana would often stop and talk to other mothers and she made a point of competing in parents' races at the school's annual sports day.

'I live for my sons. I would be lost without them'

Diana

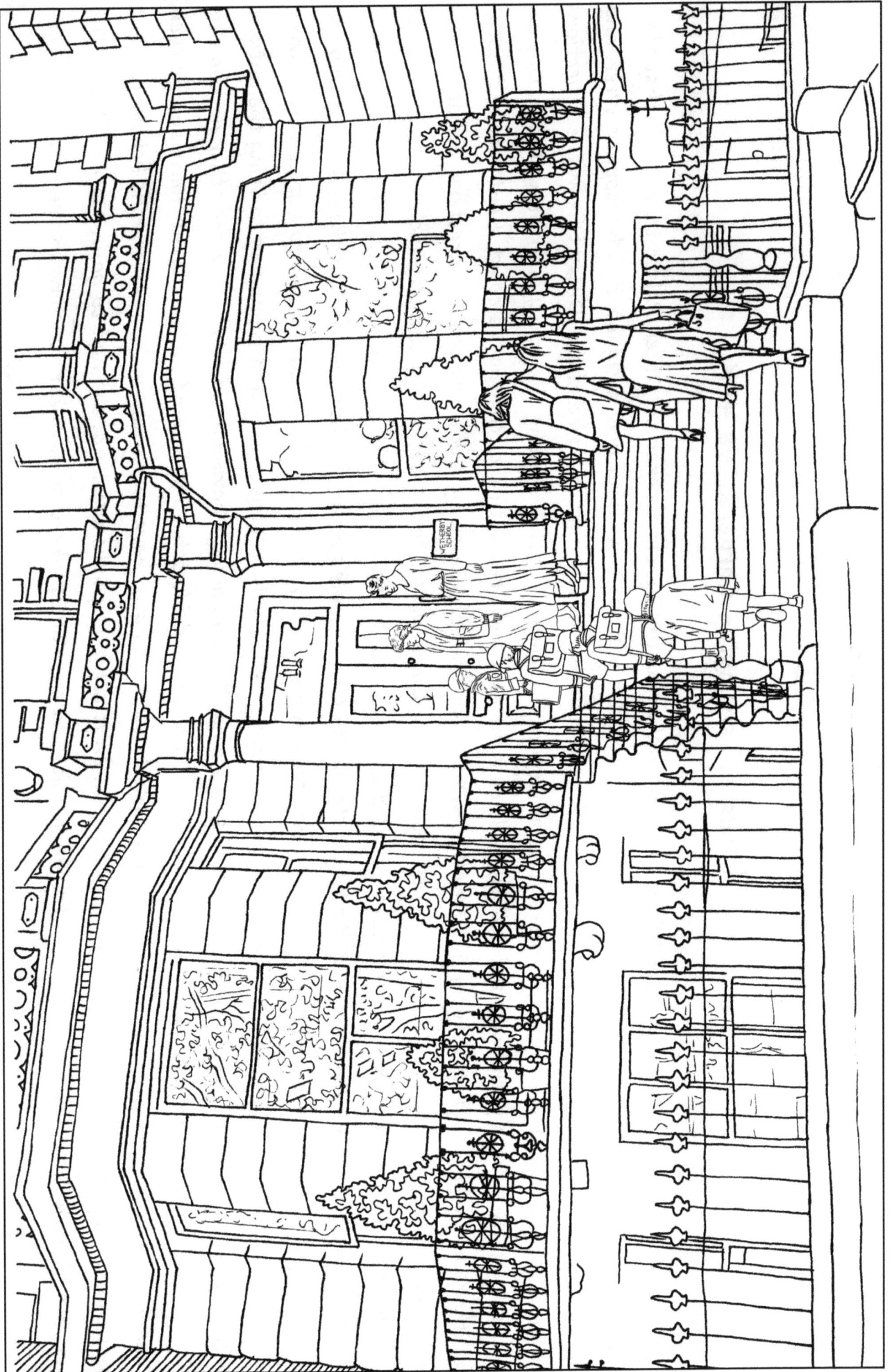

Kensington Palace, Kensington Gardens, W8 4PX

Apartments 8 and 9 were Diana and Charles's principal home until their separation. Other Palace tenants at that time were Princess Margaret and Prince Michael of Kent and his wife. The building was designed by Christopher Wren and opened in 1899. Parts of it are open to the public and couples can even get married there. Dresses from the collections of the Queen, Diana and Princess Margaret are on view in five elegant rooms. Among the many interesting things to view is the King's Staircase with walls painted by William Kent as a vivid recreation of George 1's court. Kent received £500 for the work, which depicts a lively Eighteenth Century court full of intriguing and unexpected characters. What visitors won't be able to see, however are the private rooms where Diana played with her boys .getting a much needed help once the genial Inspector Ken Wharfe got drafted in as their royal protection officer. She certainly needed it especially when it came to Harry. As Ken Wharfe says in the biography **HARRY The People's Prince**: 'When I arrived on the scene the younger royal was already showing an adventurous side not seen in his brother. You never knew quite what to expect with Harry.' He first saw the three-year-old trying to pull the stamens from a table display of lilies and managing to bring the antique vase crashing to the ground in pieces. 'Oh dear,' said Diana, 'Harry's always having accidents – only the other day he was bouncing on my bed and somehow managed to crash on to the bedside table. My framed pictures went flying and he even managed to break the glass of two of them. I'm afraid you're going to have to put up with his boisterous behavior.' That was Diana speaking as William and Harry's Mum: When it came to public speaking, she had to go in search of help. The late Sir Richard Attenborough became a frequent visitor to the palace where he gave her coaching in the art.

'When I make a speech in public, I'm nervous and when I'm nervous I giggle . . . My family are my worst critics. Rude royal relations knock my speeches'

Diana

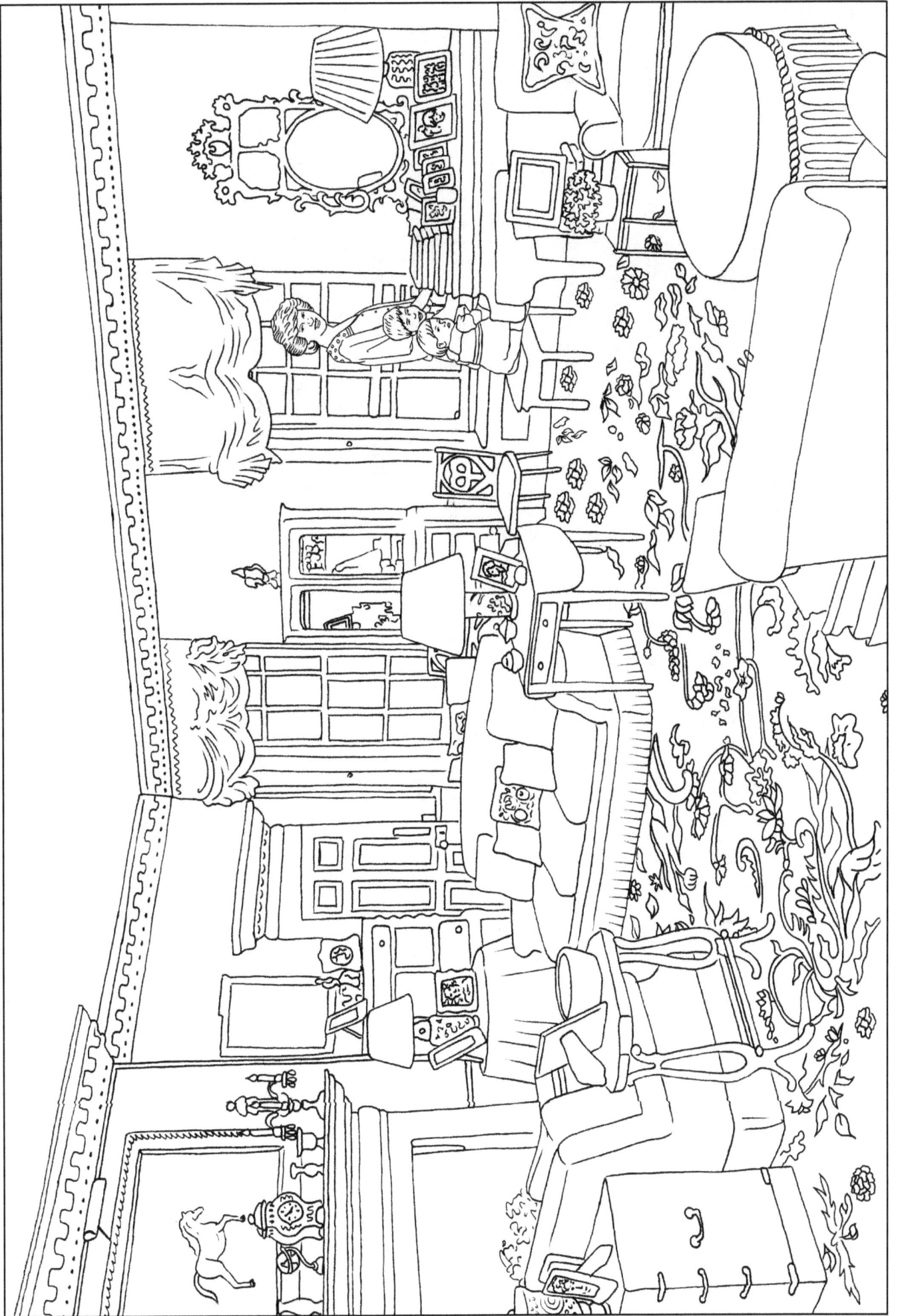

12

San Lorenzo, 22 Beauchamp Place, SW3 1NH

Just around the corner from Harrods is sited Diana's favourite restaurant and she would eat there two or three days a week, often taking William and Harry with her. Inside San Lorenzo, Diana could relax, confident in the knowledge that the natives were friendly. The restaurant's Italian owners, Mara and Lorenzo Berni, made her feel nothing if not wanted, needed and loved. Anyone choosing to eat there today can try bagging Diana's table and seek a chat with Lorenzo about his memories of the Princess. She chose the venue as a location to make her first public appearance after the-then Prime Minister, John Major, had announced in Parliament that Diana and Charles were to part. Dressed in a figure-hugging suit with a skirt short enough to be called eye-catching, the Princess clutched a son in each hand as she descended the stairs to the basement dining level. There they were greeted by Mara, a motherly figure who, among other services, collected private mail for her most famous friend after Diana grew suspicious about the Kensington Palace post room. On her way to the familiar corner table beneath giant potted palms – just beyond Andy Warhol's portrait of Marilyn Monroe – Diana made a point of stopping whenever she recognised a diner to exchange a greeting giving a clear indication that the two princes, then aged ten and eight, were the most important men in her life. On another occasion she threw a birthday party for her mother in a private upstairs dining room and had a grand piano hauled up to it for the young princes' school music teacher, a Mr Pritchard, to play Mrs Shand Kydd's favourite tunes.

'I loved Diana like a daughter. She was such a lovely person.'

Mara Berni

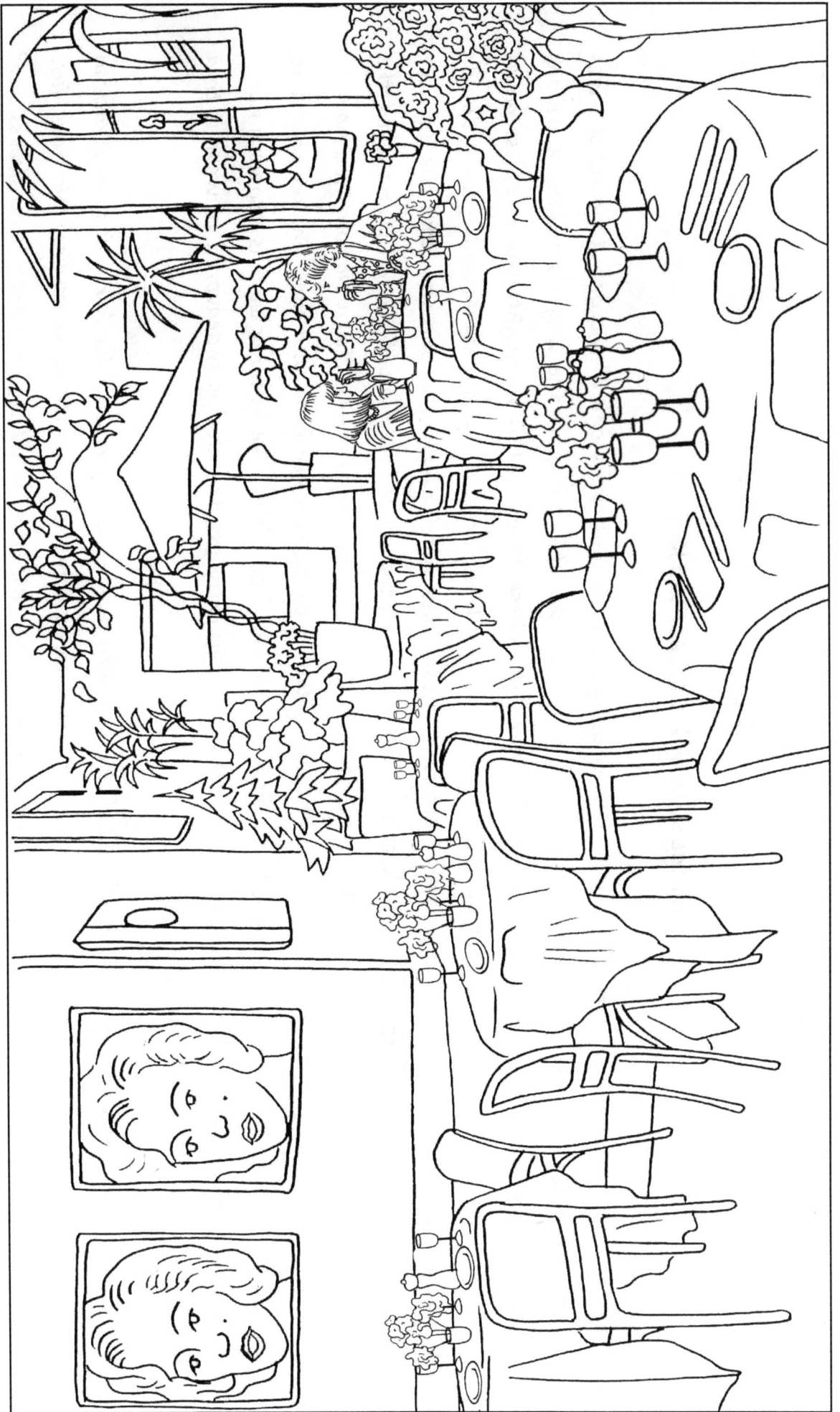

Claridge's, Brook Street, W1K 4HR

Diana was always conscious about dressing appropriately for each and every one of the grand events she was required to grace with her presence. Sometimes, however, she didn't get it quite the way her palace guardians would approve of. Eyebrows were raised at BP when she chose to wear this midnight blue strapless gown featuring a theatrical fishtail skirt of multiple tulle layers – a frock created by Murray Arbeid – for a dinner given by the President of Greece in 1986 at Mayfair's most iconic hotel, Claridge's. She also wore the Spencer tiara in apparent preference to any of those available to her in the royal collection. Although Diana loved the heavy jewel-encrusted tiara she found it painful to wear. She told her hairdresser Richard Dalton, 'You have to do something about this', so Richard had velvet lining sewn in to cushion her head and used knicker elastic to keep it stable. He says, 'We would pull her hair over the top and blend it in. The Spencer tiara is also very noisy. It rattles from all the pearls so it drove her a little mad.' Nevertheless, she always endeavored to wear it to a function she considered appropriate.

When the Princess asked a Papal official charged with making arrangements for her visit to the Vatican to meet Pope John Paul II what were the rules about how she should dress, he replied: 'No rules, just don't clash with his Holiness – he'll be all in white, long dress, long sleeves . . .'

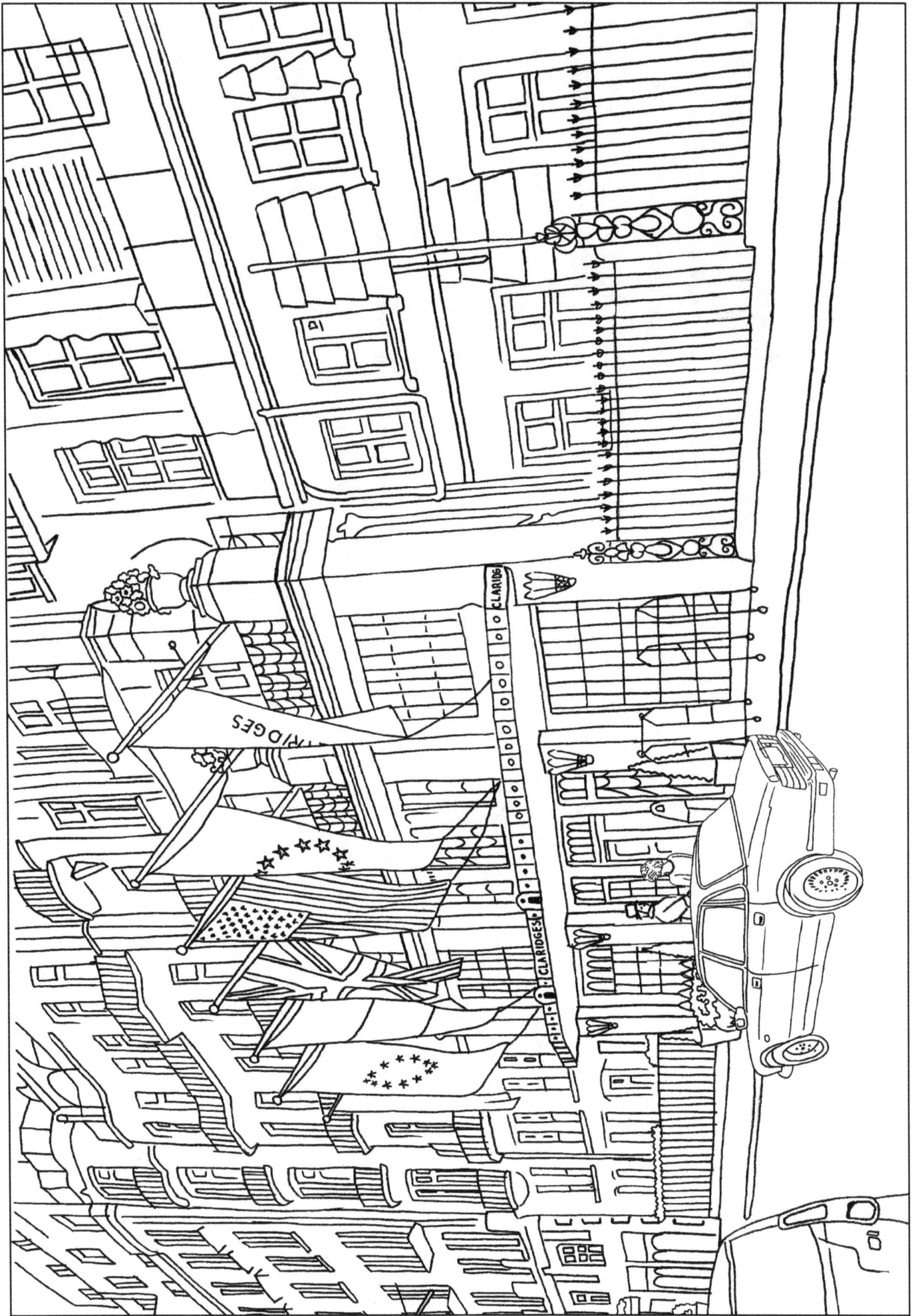

Sticky Fingers, 1A Phillimore Gardens, W8 7QB

When William and Harry were very young Diana would not allow them to come back to Kensington Palace from kindergarten in North London to be spoiled by the servants. She would say, 'What do you want to do, boys?' and they'd say, 'Can we have a burger?' Royal protection officer Inspector Ken Wharfe recalls, 'We'd go down to Sticky Fingers, Bill Wyman's place near Kensington High Street, and then to Marks & Spencer's and pick up something else from the food department there. It was her way of getting out of Kensington Palace and introducing her children to the real world. They loved all that but Prince Charles couldn't understand it. When we got back to the palace one day, he asked, "Where have you been?" One of the boys replied, "Oh Papa, we've been to Kensington High Street and this great burger bar that belongs to one of the Rolling Stones and then we went to Marks & Spencer." Charles turned to Diana and said, "Why do you take them to a burger bar when we've got a chef here to cook food for them?" He couldn't see it. Diana would just raise her eyebrows and say, "Oh, for God's sake." They just weren't on the same wavelength. What she was doing without any support from him was educating her children in a very Twentieth Century way.'

'It is vital that the Monarchy keeps in touch with the people. It's what I try and do.'

Diana

FINGERS
THE EXCITEMENT, ENTERTAINMENT AND MUSIC OF TEENAGE AMERICA!
Starring
THE BEACH BOYS
CHUCK BERRY
JAMES BROWN AND THE FLAMES
THE BARBARIANS
MARVIN GAYE
GERRY AND THE PACEMAKERS
LESLEY GORE
JAN AND DEAN
BILLY J. KRAMER AND THE DAKOTAS
SMOKEY ROBINSON AND THE MIRACLES
THE SUPREMES
THE ROLLING STONES in
THE FIRST ANNUAL
T-A-M-I SHOW
ELECTRONOVISION
STONES IN THE PARK

15

Royal Opera House, Bow Street, WC2E 9DD

As a child, Diana's ambition was to be a ballerina but she grew too tall. She took Prince Charles by surprise in 1985 by slipping away from their box at the Royal Opera House and turning up on stage where she danced with Wayne Sleep to Billy Joel's Uptown Girl. The Prince had no idea that his wife had been taking dance lessons from the diminutive ballet star. It turned out she had been a regular visitor to his mews house close to Kensington Palace where he would cook modest meals for her. 'We had a lot of laughs,' said Sleep. 'You'd never expect her to be that funny.' Their Opera House performance drew eight curtain calls and after the final one Sleep urged her to bow to Prince Charles in the Royal Box but Diana said, 'I'm not bowing to him, he's my hubby.' Earlier that year she put her dance lessons to good use setting America alight when footage was shown of her gliding around the White House ballroom with John Travolta. They danced to the Saturday Night Fever music at a gala dinner hosted by Ronald and Nancy Reagan.

'Diana told me she doesn't have time to dance any more, and that's sad because she loves to dance.'

Harold King of the London City Ballet

Kaspia, 18 Bruton Place, W1J 6LY (now Bellamy's)

When Diana fancied a quiet gossip with her trusted friend Hayat Palumbo (wife of Lord Palumbo – the controversial property developer who has openly clashed with Prince Charles) they would sit behind the pink geraniums in this most discreet of eateries situated in a quiet street off Berkeley Square –that, of course, is the place where the nightingales once sang. It was probably here that the two conspired with Diana's even-closer friend, Lucia Flecha de Lima, wife of the Brazilian ambassador to Britain, to venture on a shopping trip to Paris. During the trip – and to the courtiers' consternation back home – she enjoyed a cheeky lobster and sea bass lunch with the French actor Gerard Depardieu according to the biography, **Diana's Nightmare: The Family.** Incidentally, the restaurant is the only place in London where Diana's mother-in-law, Her Majesty the Queen, has eaten in public.

'I don't go by the rule book. I lead from the heart not the head'

Diana speaking about her impulsive actions

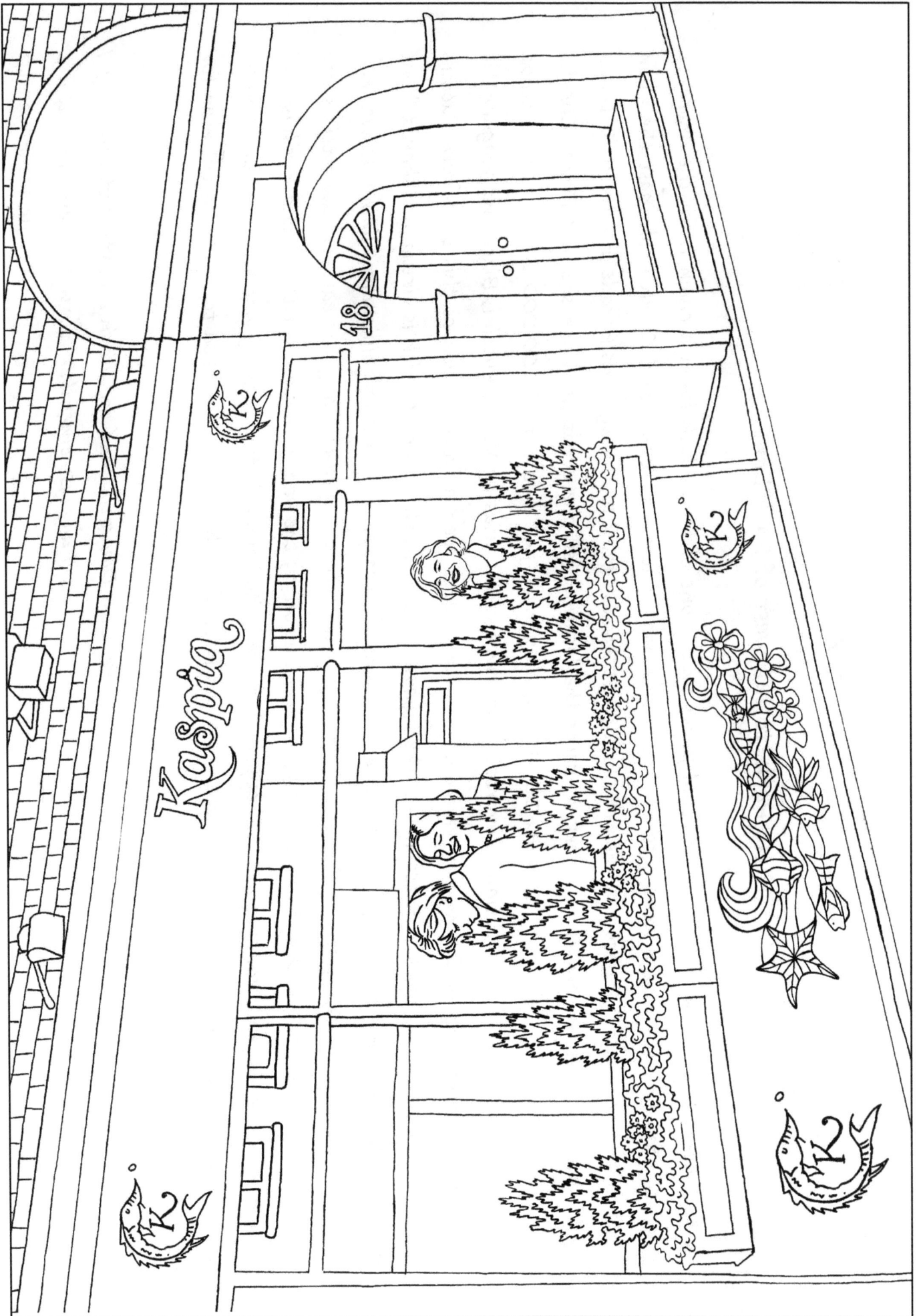

Hyde Park, to the west of Park Lane

At 350 acres this is one of the largest royal parks and is one of four which form a chain from the entrance of Kensington Palace through Kensington Gardens and, via Hyde Park Corner and Green Park, past the main entrance to Buckingham Palace and then on through St James's Park to Horseguards Parade in Whitehall. Diana would probably best remember the Park as being the location for one event at which she and Prince Charles were not the stars of the show. On July 30, 1991, they were just two out of 100,000 admirers who stood in the pouring rain to watch Luciano Pavarotti perform twenty arias by Verdi, Puccini, Bizet and Wagner. He dedicated his rendering of Donna non vidi mai – 'I have never seen a woman such as this one' from Pucini's opera Manon Lescaut, to the Princess. It was the biggest concert in the Park (which is virtually a shared front garden to Kensington Palace and the neighbouring mansions occupied by Russian billionaires lining its western flank) – since the Rolling Stones performed there to an audience of 75,000 two years earlier. Pavarotti's show should have attracted 250,000 but many people were put off by the bad weather. Not Diana and her husband though, they were keen Pavarotti fans and appeared to be quite happy getting soaking wet and laughed when he said he should have sung Singing In The Rain. She said later that she would have liked to ask the great man for his autograph but was 'too shy'.

'Princess Diana touched my life in an extraordinary way. I will always remember her with deep love and joy.'

Luciano Pavarotti

18

Vogue House, Hanover Square, W1S 1JU

This was the work base of Diana's friend Anna Harvey who, for a time, was the Princess's semi-official wardrobe advisor. It was also the venue where she had many a heated argument over what she should wear on certain occasions once she had acquired sufficient self-confidence to become mistress of her own image! At the beginning her look was 'fairy tale princess' – the embodiment of every little girl's fantasy of what it meant to be a princess. Diana and Ms Harvey first met in 1980 when she was plain Lady Diana Spencer and Ms Harvey was working in the fashion department at British Vogue. It was the magazine's then-editor, Beatrix Miller, who chose Anna to work with Diana. Once she'd got over the fairy-tale-princess stage, Diana became something of a Laura-Ashley-sheathed Sloane, and it was left to Anna to turn her into an international style icon enlisting the help of such designers as Catherine Walker, Jacques Azagury and Versace. It was through a photo shoot for Vogue that Diana met the man who was to become her favourite photographer, Patrick Demarchalier.

'Clothes are for the job. They've got to be practical. Sometimes I can be a little outrageous which is quite nice . . . but only sometimes.'

Diana

Harvey Nichols, 109–125 Knightsbridge, SW1X 7RJ

This is the store where Diana was a frequent shopper. She particularly liked the work of London College of Fashion-educated designer Azagury and was often to be seen admiring his New Romantics collection there. The store's first floor was a particular favourite with the Princess and she never skimped when stocking her wardrobe with designs by such internationally known fashion names as Ralph Lauren, Donna Koran, Isaac Mizrahi, Sonia Rykiel, Jean-Paul Gaultier, Claude Montana, Dolce & Gabanna and Moschino. An easygoing place, Harvey Nicks, as she called it, offered a private suite where Diana could be shown and allowed to try on clothes, but she often preferred to wander round the departments mingling with other customers as she picked out her choices. She was, of course, aware that the attention she received was greater than that afforded to any other celebrity – particularly when she enjoyed a glass of champaigne in the bar.

'Do you want them to be looking at you or me?' Diana when dancer Wayne Sleep suggested she might like to sit in the audience rather than watch him perform from the theatre wings

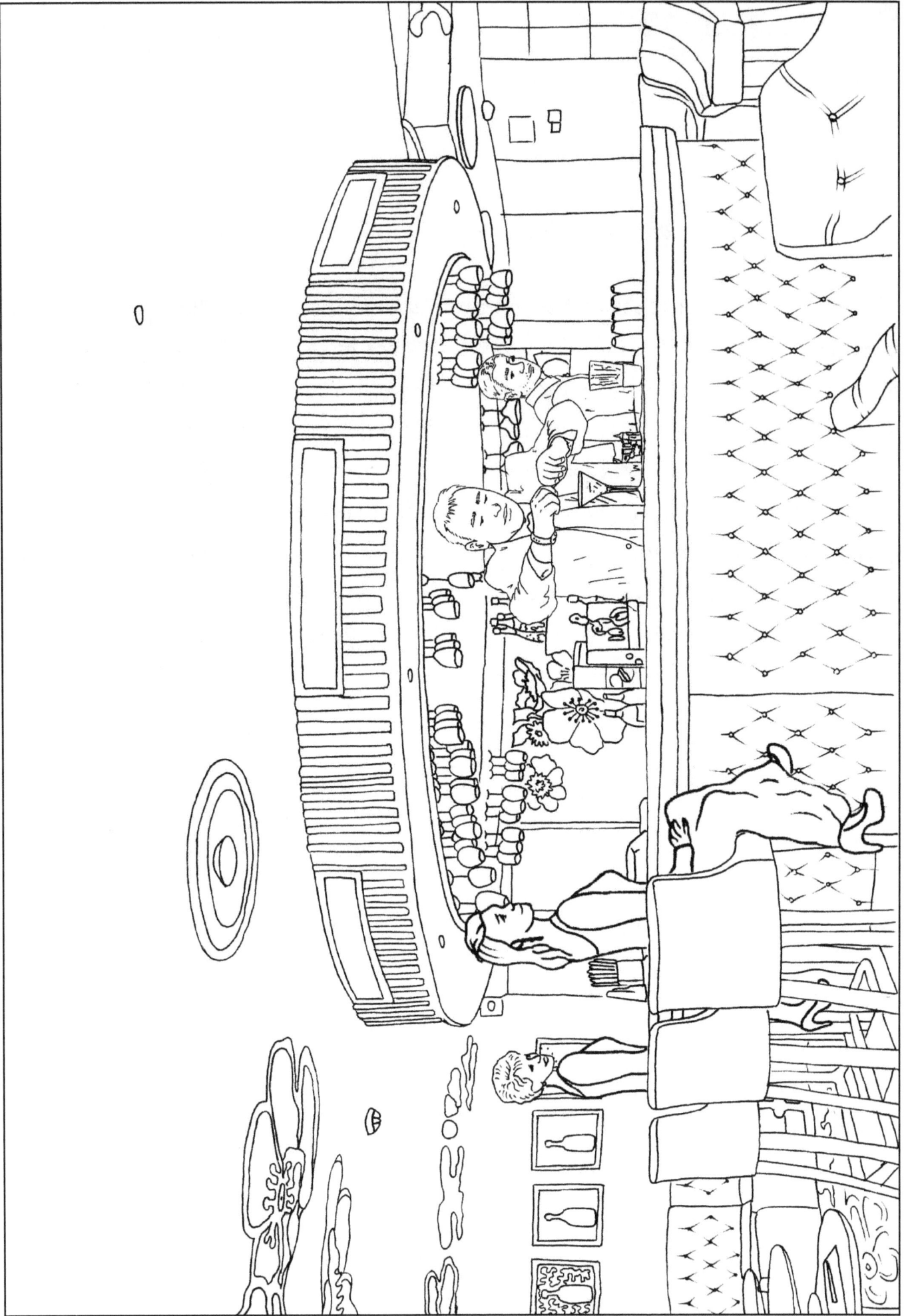

Lanesborough Hotel, Hyde Park Corner, SW1X 7TA

Though they had been separated for three years, Diana and Charles both attended a Christmas party for the staff of St James's Palace at this hotel close to Kensington Place in December 1995. Diana had just returned from a triumphant trip to New York but was upset over a newspaper photograph of Charles giving their son's nanny, Tiggy Legge-Bourke, a friendly peck on the cheek on the ski slopes. Mistakenly believing that Tiggy was having an affair with the man she was still married to, Diana made a sarcastic comment to the young nanny. As a result, Tiggy consulted libel lawyers and the Queen's Private Secretary Sir Robert Fellowes (he was also the Princess's brother-in-law) wrote to assure Diana that her fears were groundless. The matter was settled out of court at Diana's expense and she continued to be on friendly terms with, -'er - almost everyone else who worked for her.

'Familiarity breeds contempt'
Prince Philip on Diana consorting with below-stairs staff

Vanderbilt Racquet Club, 31 Sterne Street, W12 8AB

A keen player since her teenage years, Diana joined this club in Shepherd's Bush ostensibly to play tennis but she found that membership also plugged her into another network . . . fellow members included Mick Jagger, Charlton Heston and Richard Branson's mother Eve, but it was women's number one seed Steffi Graf who the Princess most enjoyed competing with at the club. Diana endeared herself to the club's director, Charles Swallow, by insisting she pay the £650 entrance fee and annual subscription of £550 which would otherwise have been available on a complimentary basis since her name meant future business for any commercial enterprise it was linked with. Furthermore, according to the biography, DIANA: **Always there**, she made no objection to photographs of herself chatting with other members being included in the montages which adorned the club hallway.

'She was very good, she surprised me. She has a good serve and forehand but her backhand needs a little work.'

Steffi Graf on Diana's tennis performance

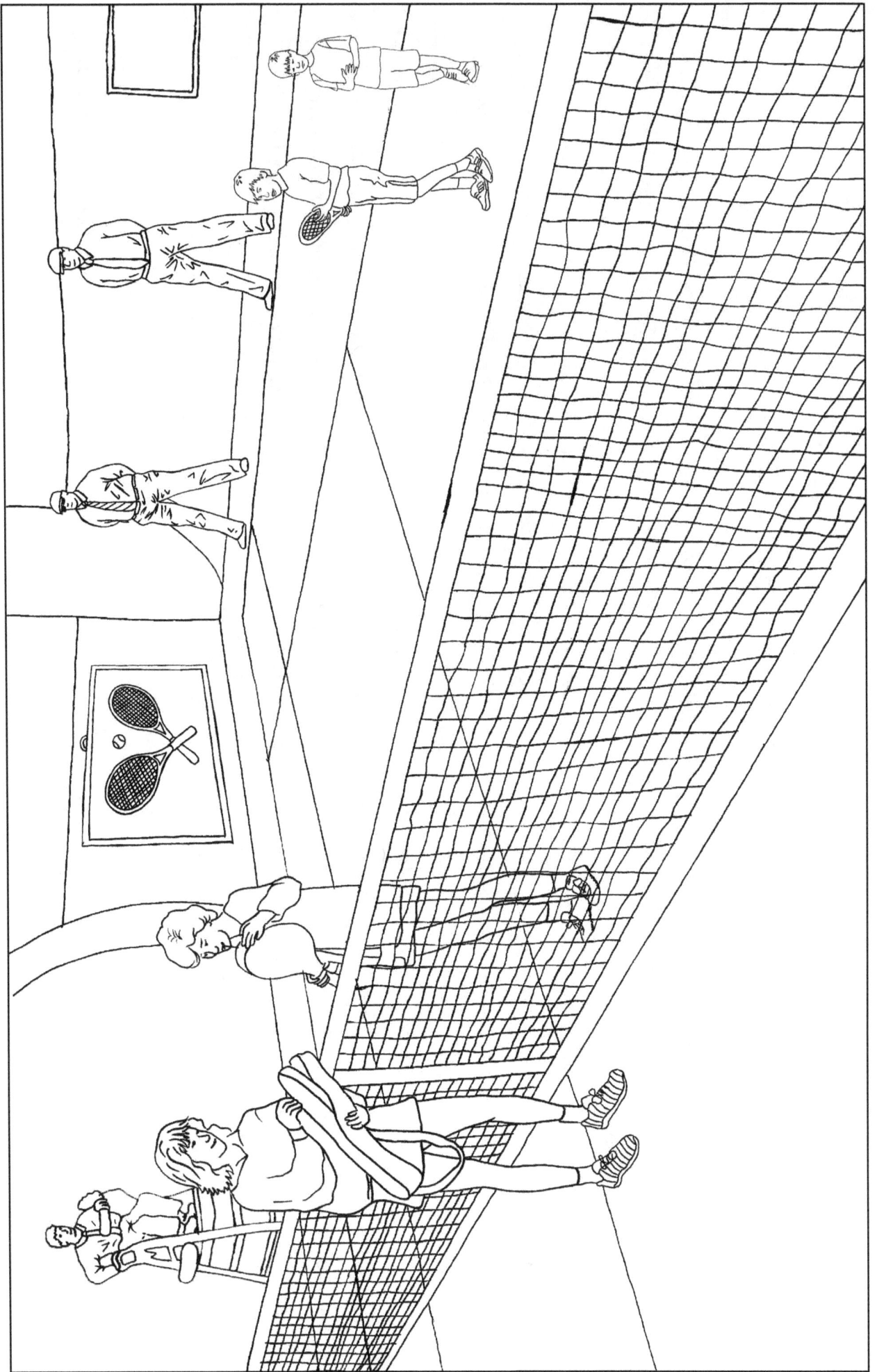

Royal Vauxhall Tavern, 372 Kennington Lane, SE11 5HY

Having spent an afternoon at Kenny Everett's flat drinking champagne and watching TV re-runs of The Golden Girls with the disc jockey, Queen frontman Freddie Mercury and comedy actress Cleo Rocos, Princess Diana (in mischievous mood) agreed to accompany the trio to the Royal Vauxhall having been warned in advance that it was one of London's oldest and best known gay venues. She was promised 'an evening of surprise entertainment'. Diana went dressed in an army jacket, cap and sunglasses loaned to her by Everett. Cleo was later to say, 'When we walked in to the Tavern, we felt she was obviously Princess Diana and would be discovered at any minute, but people just seemed to blank her. She sort of disappeared but she loved it.' Diana was able to order drinks undetected in the venue where the regular clientele included the actor Sir Ian McKellen and the TV host Graham Norton. Ms Rocos said she did not know whether Diana was propositioned in the bar in her guise as a male model, but added: 'She did look like a beautiful young man. Never has going to a bar been quite so exhilarating and such fun. When we made our exit to grab a cab, the jolly queens queuing outside unknowingly waved back as their queen of hearts waved goodbye to them. My lasting memory of that day is of watching Diana, Kenny and Freddie dancing round his lounge to the Gypsy Kings, each waving one of Kenny's feather dusters in the air.'

'I have been acting the biggest role of my career for ten years. I should be in movies'

Diana

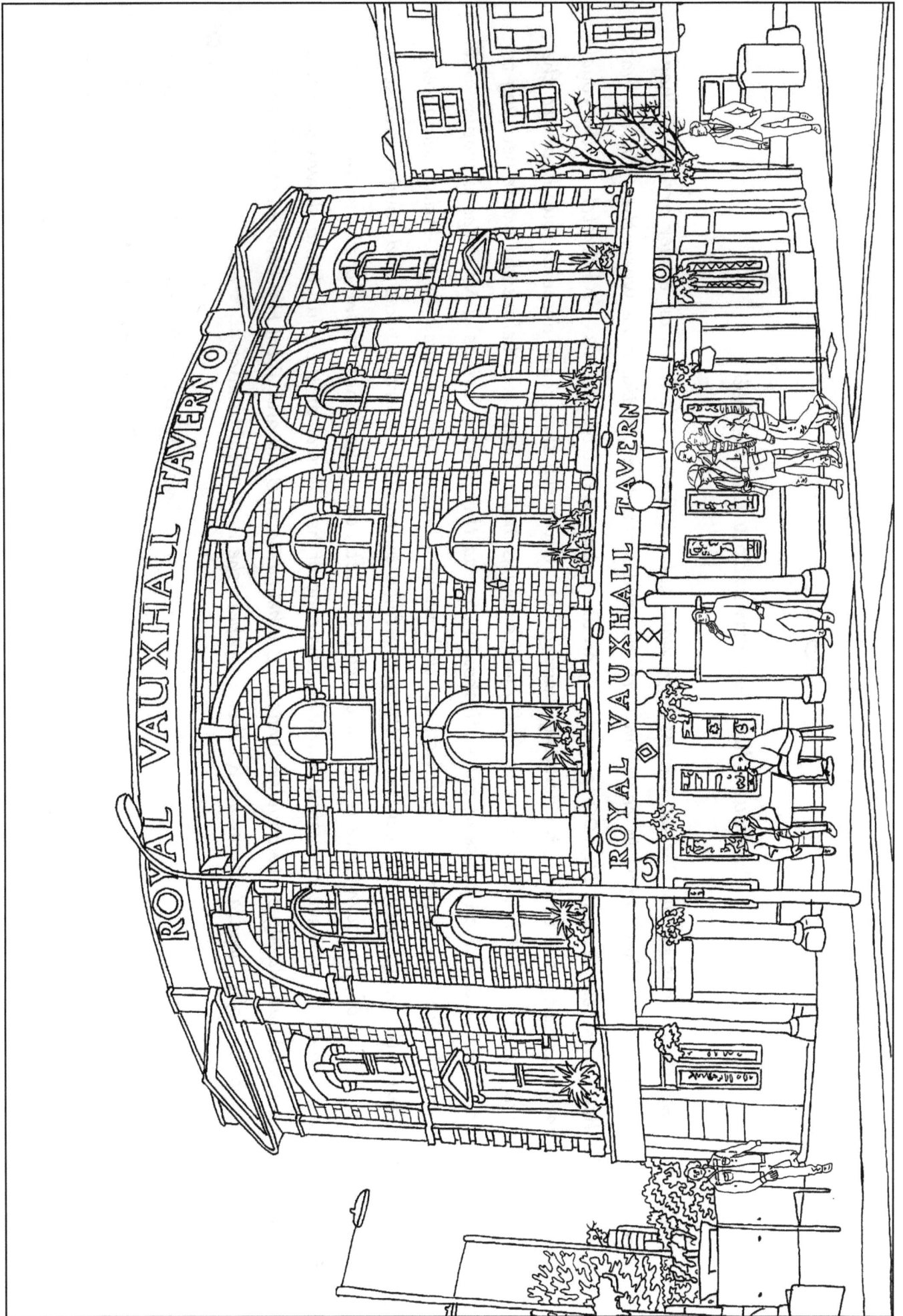

23

The Harbour Club, Watermeadow Lane, SW6

Despite its name the club is not in Chelsea but its high walls actually protect it from an edgier area of Fulham where the pubs' customers have little in common with the club's clientele. At the time when the Princess was working out here membership cost £2,400 followed by an annual payment of £1,158 – no stretch on the royal purse and Diana did not have to join the lengthy waiting list. On entry she would descend four floors to the basement where a receptionist handed her two fluffy white towels and a locker key before she made her way to a changing room. She would often pause at the noticeboard to read the latest offerings of New Age therapies and remedies. Having changed she went to the fitness centre's main workout area where weight-lifting equipment is arranged around the walls with the centre of the room filled by ranks of exercise bikes and rowing and step machines. At the front of the room there is a bank of television sets, each one tuned to one of the main channels. Surreally, Diana would often have to watch morning coverage of her arrival at the Club being shown on news channels. She worked out mainly on two weight machines labelled Total Body and Total Hip before retiring to the restaurant lounge for coffee and a natter with other members she had come to know.

'Working out helps me deal with the stress – and there's plenty of that in my job.'

Diana

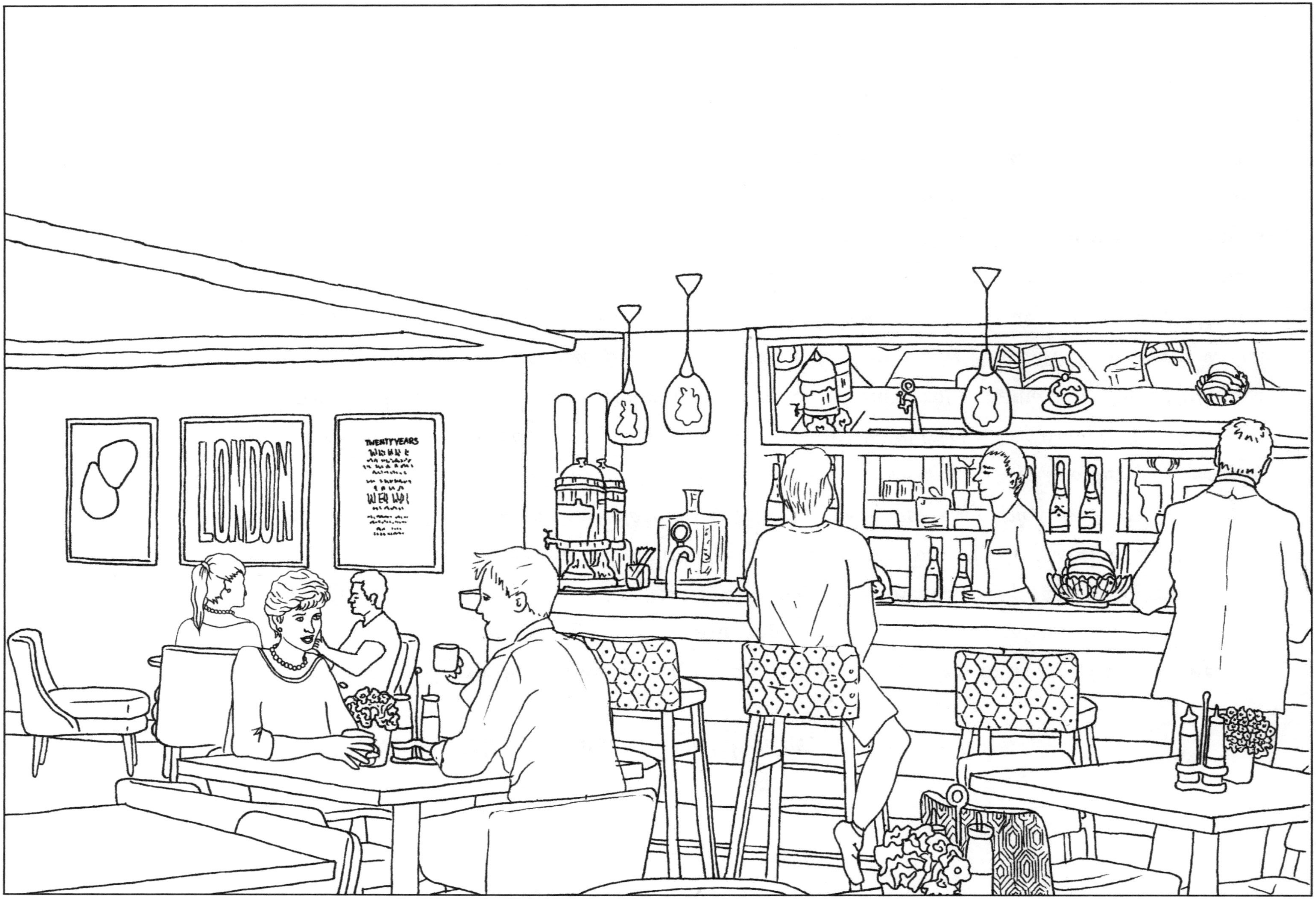
LONDON
TWENTY YEARS

24

No 6 Walton Street, Knightsbridge, SW3 1RE

Diana conducted her romance with the handsome Army officer Major James Hewitt in this house owned by Lorenzo and Mara Berni, proprietors of her favourite restaurant, San Lorenzo, which was situated nearby. The Princess had flowers, champagne and delicious delicacies delivered from nearby Harrods ahead of her cosy meetings with the Major at No.6 their-then secret bolt hole. Finding places for private meetings was always difficult for the Princess – she did not trust the Palace and, believing she was being spied on there, even had floorboards taken up in a sweep for electronic bugs. So it was understandable that Diana had her confidential mail – including Hewitt's love letters – delivered to San Lorenzo. Mara would take her mail to the house in Walton Street where she could read it in private. Royal protector Ken Wharfe told the author Chris Hutchins: 'James Hewitt wasn't a bad man but he dreamed of settling down with Diana in a house in the country which was never an option. Diana told me she met James in London in the summer of 1986 at a party given by her lady-in-waiting Hazel West. He was charming and likeable. He was also her riding instructor who offered to help her overcome her fear of riding. By 1987 James had become her biggest source of comfort and support. Charles knew about the relationship but chose to turn a blind eye.' The Princess and the Household Cavalry officer got on famously from the start and the provision of this Knightsbridge love nest afforded them time to get to know each other better.

'I do like men in uniform.'

Diana

25

Great Ormond Street Hospital for Children, London WC1N 3JH

Originally known as The Hospital for Sick Children, Britain's most famous medical centre for infants opened its doors at 49 Great Ormond Street on Valentine's Day 1852 with 10 beds. Princess Diana followed many famous supporters including Queen Victoria, Charles Dickens and J.M. Barrie, through its doors. Playwright Barrie donated the rights of Peter Pan to the hospital. Diana was a regular visitor. On both official and private visits to GOSH she sought out the shyest child for her special attention and with Prince Charles she launched the Wishing Well Appeal, which raised £50 million.

'Diana showed great compassion and understanding. She seemed very sad when she was told how badly the children needed treatment.'

Dr Lidio Russo, Leukemia Specialist

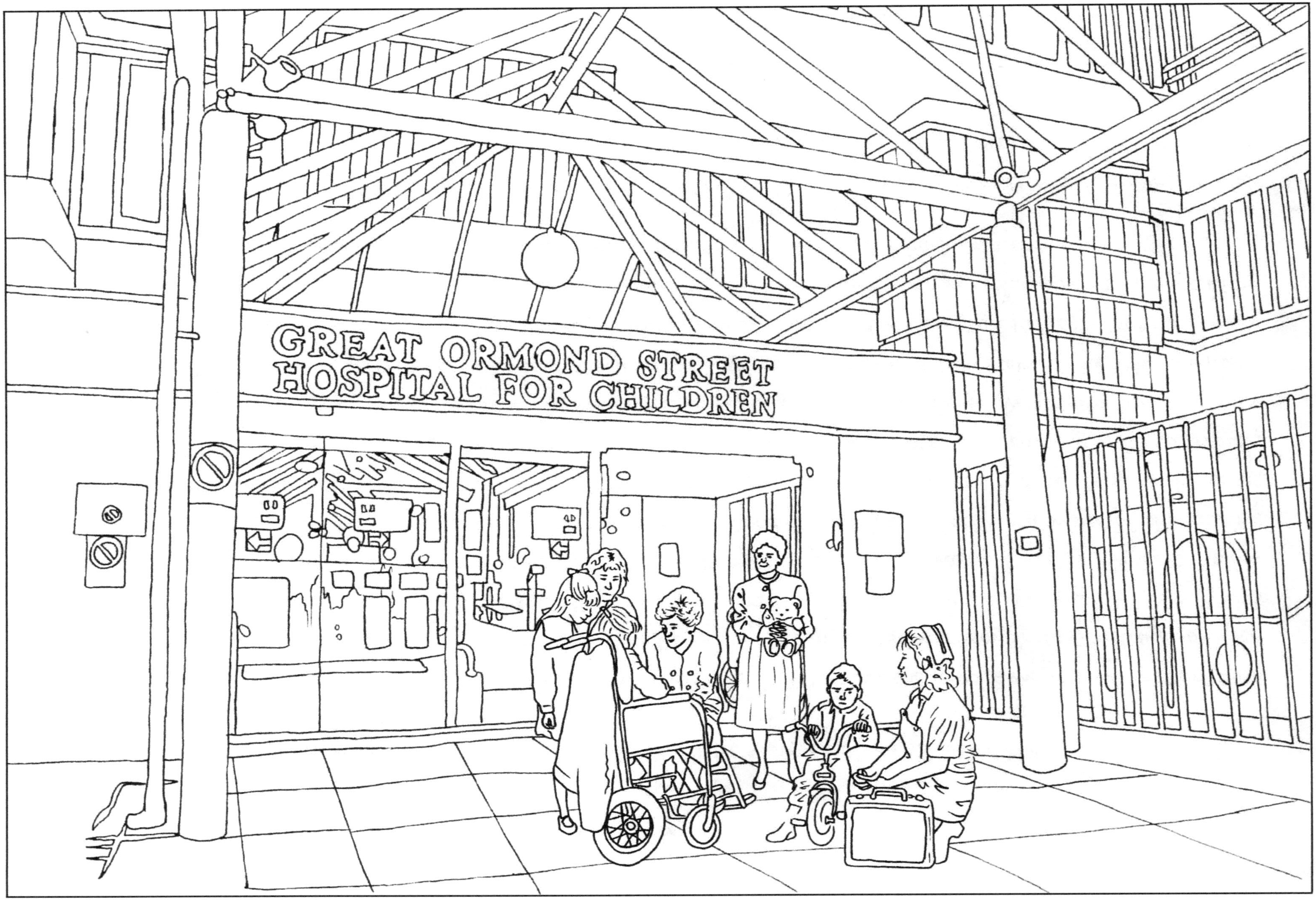
GREAT ORMOND STREET
HOSPITAL FOR CHILDREN

26

Royal Brompton Hospital, Sydney Street, Chelsea, SW3 6NP

Children were her delight – friends say Diana always wanted a little girl – and she always made a beeline for those she felt most needed her attention. One of those was eight–year–old Danielle Stephenson from Southend–on–Sea whose story dramatically illustrates Diana's concern. When a nurse told Danielle that a very famous person was coming to see her she guessed it was going to be the footballer Alan Shearer. It was in fact the Princess paying a private visit to see a patient in another ward and Danielle stood by the lift to catch a glimpse of the visiting VIP. But not for long. Within minutes of Diana appearing she was sitting on Danielle's bed laughing with her at the antics of the stars in the television show Absolutely Fabulous. It became the first of her many visits to the girl and when Danielle was asked what they had in common she replied, 'We talked about everything and anything. When I told her about my guinea pigs she said she used to have guinea pigs and hamsters.' The schoolgirl and her mother subsequently took up an invitation to join the Princess for tea at Kensington Palace – but they were not the only ones. It was at the Royal Brompton that she met the love of her life, heart surgeon Dr Hasnat Khan who she had her butler smuggle into the palace hidden under a blanket in the back of a car.

'She was just like one of the girls. She came in, put her handbag down and chatted to me like an old friend.'

A hospital patient

27

The Serpentine Gallery, set close to the eponymous artificial lake in Hyde Park

Resplendent in what was to be described as 'a sexy Revenge Dress', Diana was being driven to a charity show at the Serpentine Gallery in 1993 when she asked her chauffeur, Simon Solari, to park nearby so that she could compose herself. It was pointless. This was the day on which her husband was to be seen on television owning up to adultery. Half an hour after the performance began Diana fled the theatre claiming she had a migraine. But next day she was back on form, joking to another charity audience about the growing rumours of her being mentally unstable. 'Ladies and gentlemen,' she said, 'you are very lucky to have your patron here today. I was supposed to have had my head down the loo all day, I am supposed to be dragged off the moment I leave here by men in white coats. But if it's all right by you, I thought I might postpone my nervous breakdown for a more appropriate moment.' By the end of the year, however, the strain was genuine and Diana was at low ebb. It was then that she shocked her admirers by announcing her withdrawal from much of public life and her role as the figurehead of many charities.

'The kindness and affection from the public have carried me through some of the most difficult periods.'

Diana

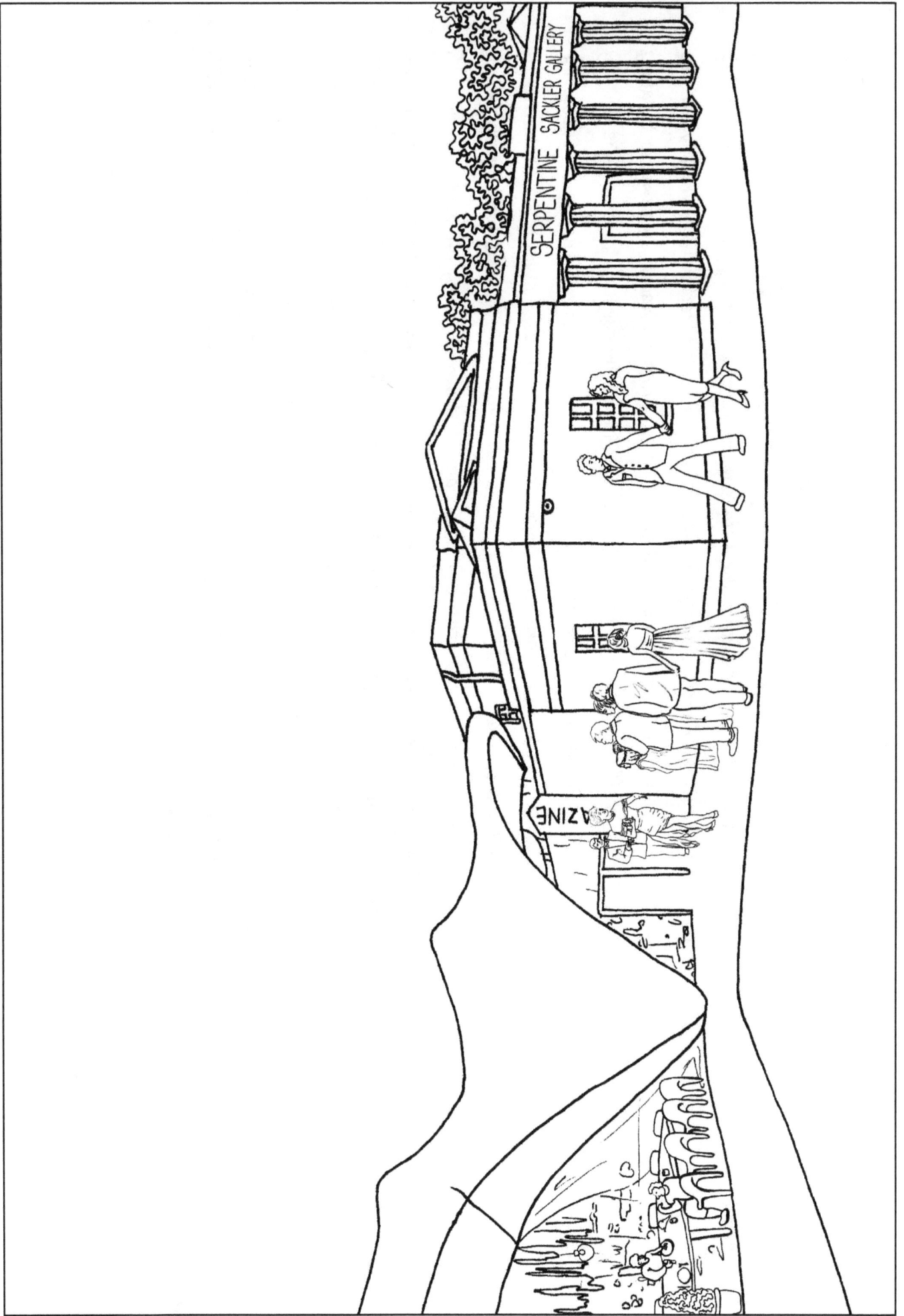

28

Harrods, 87–135 Brompton Road, SW1X 7XL

Diana and her Sloane Ranger friends called it 'Horrids' and she said she preferred to shop at nearby 'Harvey Nicks' but the decorous Harrods – long the Royal Family's favourite shopping mall – offered wares which were too tempting to ignore. Steeped in custom from the most important of all VIPs, Harrods had a system for dealing with the special ones. A call from Palace staff would alert Harrods staff to Diana's impending arrival (she usually got a lady-in-waiting to phone ahead) and when she arrived she would be met by the Director of Customer Services who would remain in attendance throughout her visit. Harrods was, of course, owned by Mohammed Al Fayed, the father of Dodi Fayed, who died with Diana in the Paris car crash at the end of August 1997. Following their deaths Al Fayed commissioned a bronze statue of the pair of them dancing on a beach beneath the wings of an albatross which was displayed in the store. Another memorial he had placed at the base of the Egyptian Escalator featured photographs of them both and a display case containing a wine glass smudged with lipstick from Diana's last dinner and what was described as an engagement ring Dodi purchased the day before they lost their lives. The Princess's friendship with Dodi enabled her to use the Al Fayed organization's helicopter and aeroplane to travel out of the country for a holiday on the Al Fayed yacht, rather than using commercial flights from Heathrow where the Press was impossible to avoid, but it was Dr Hasnat Khan she was in love with (see Royal Brompton Hospital) at the time.

'People do make life easier for me when I'm on the spend. What's to complain about?'

Diana

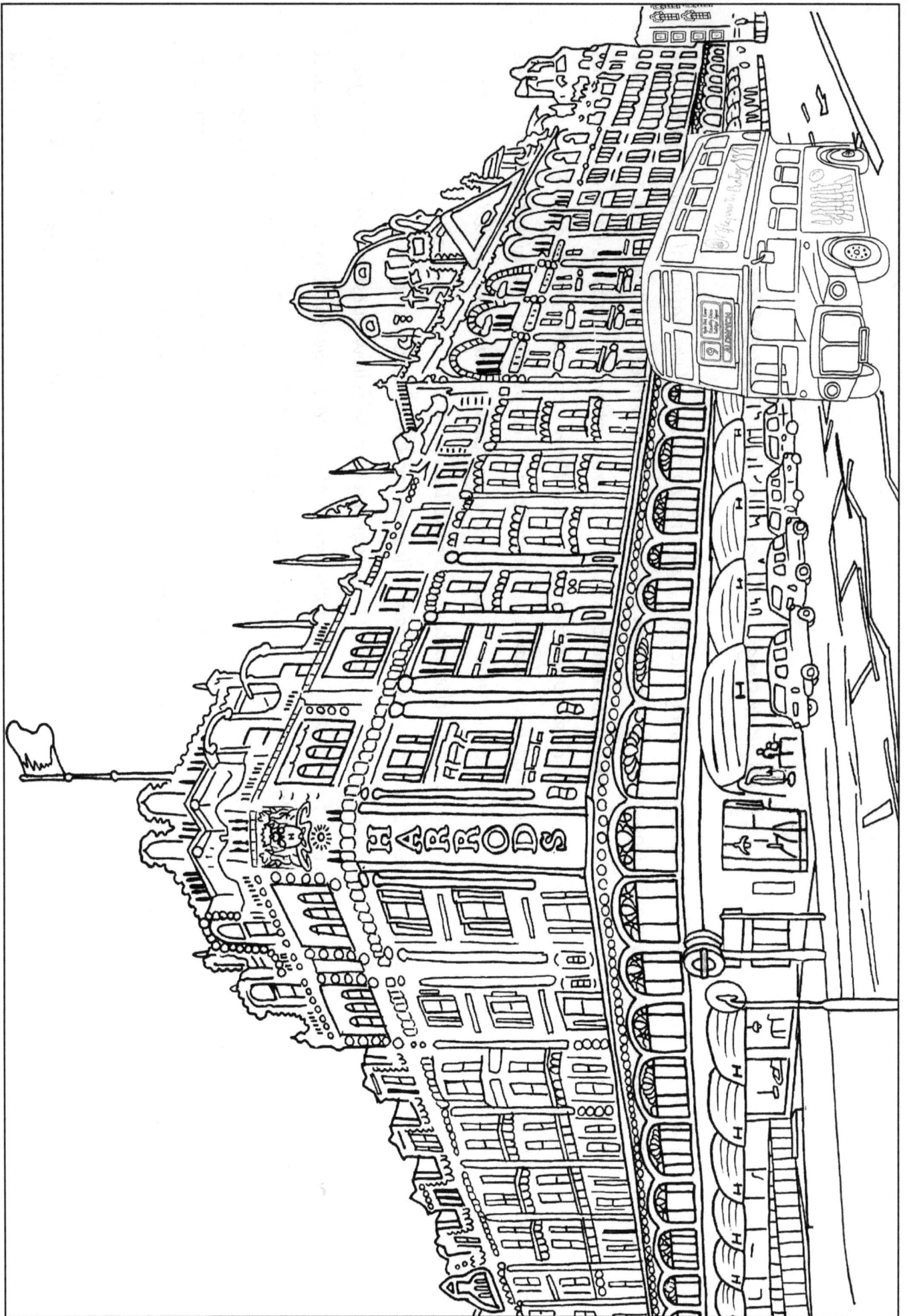

29

The Royal Albert Hall, Kensington Gore, London SW7 2AP

Diana wore a spectacular, low-cut blue silk dress by Jacques Azagury to the English National Ballet's premiere performance of Derek Deane's production of the ballet Swan Lake at the Royal Albert Hall on June 3, 1997. She had asked Azagury for 'something special' having been told that Deane's production of what has been acclaimed as Tchaikovsky's greatest work, would be amazing and would feature no less than sixty ballerina swans. She was also wearing a fabulous new necklace which glittered with diamonds and South Sea pearls and which she had helped design. Once the matching ear rings – which had not been ready for the occasion – had been added, the jewellery was named the Swan Lake Suite to commemorate the entertainment Diana was enjoying on the only night she ever wore it. The three pieces were later sold to an American collector for £362,000. After the show which she described as 'The most magical ballet experience of my life' Diana agreed to join fellow guest Mohamed Al Fayed, the colourful tycoon who owned Harrods, for supper. During the meal Al Fayed suggested that the Princess and her sons, William and Harry, might like to holiday with him and his family in St Tropez. She accepted and it was there that she was romanced by Al Fayed's son, Dodi. After the holiday she returned to the South of France with Dodi and it was from there they ventured on their ill-fated trip to Paris where the Princess and the tycoon's son were to die in a car crash on July 31 – just 58 days after her magical Swan Lake night.

'I just like laughing. I'm a normal person, hopefully, who loves life.'

Diana

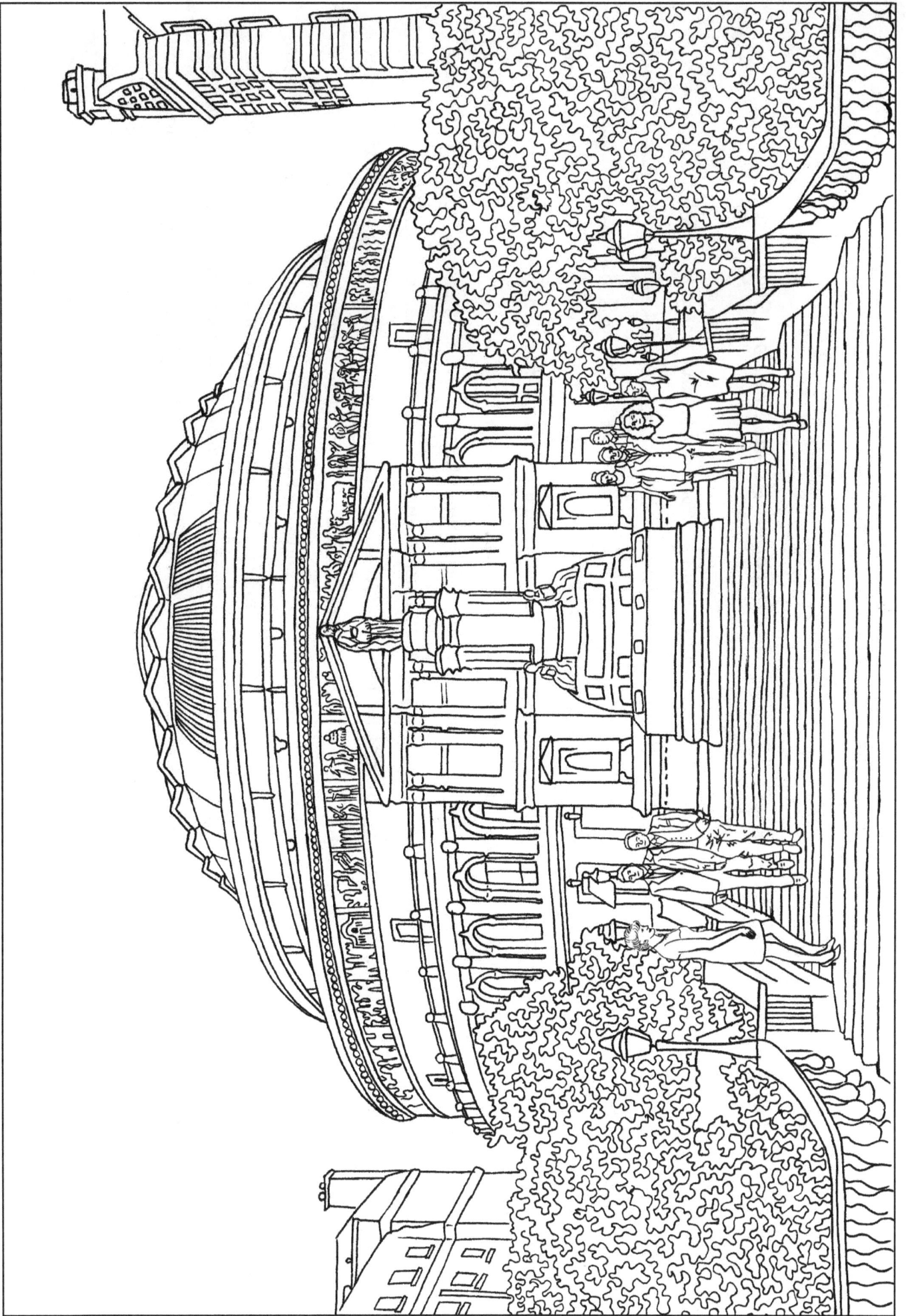

30

The Chapel Royal, St James's Palace, Marlborough Road, London SW1A 1BS

On 31 August 1997 Prince Charles and Diana's sisters Lady Sarah McCorquodale and Lady Jane Fellowes escorted the late Princess's body back from Paris to the United Kingdom. The Princess was taken to the Chapel Royal adjacent to St James Palace where she lay in state for five days before being taken to Kensington Palace. The then Prime Minister, Tony Blair, pressed the Queen to fly back to London from Balmoral, her Scottish summer retreat, in order to join in the tumult of public grief. The outpouring of love for Diana proved conclusively that the vast majority of people adored her unreservedly and were grief-stricken at her loss. The very public devotion to her memory brought home to the Royal Family their own shortcomings. It also effectively shamed the scandalmongers into silence and ended — for a while at least — the sniping about her private life which had intensified following her separation from Charles in 1992. It was in his apartment at this palace that Charles sat Diana down for a tea-time meeting to discuss the inevitable divorce. Once they had brokered she telephoned the Queen to ask for an announcement of their plans to legally end the marriage — a request which Her Majesty had no hesitation in agreeing to. It was on 15 July 1996 that the Prince was granted a decree nisi which was made absolute at 10.27 am on August 28. It is appropriate that at the time both were in places they adored — albeit hundreds of miles apart. Charles was at Balmoral with William and Harry maintaining his connection with long-term mistress, Camilla Parker Bowles; Diana was at the London studios of the English National Ballet.

'There were three of us in this marriage, so it was a bit crowded.'

Diana

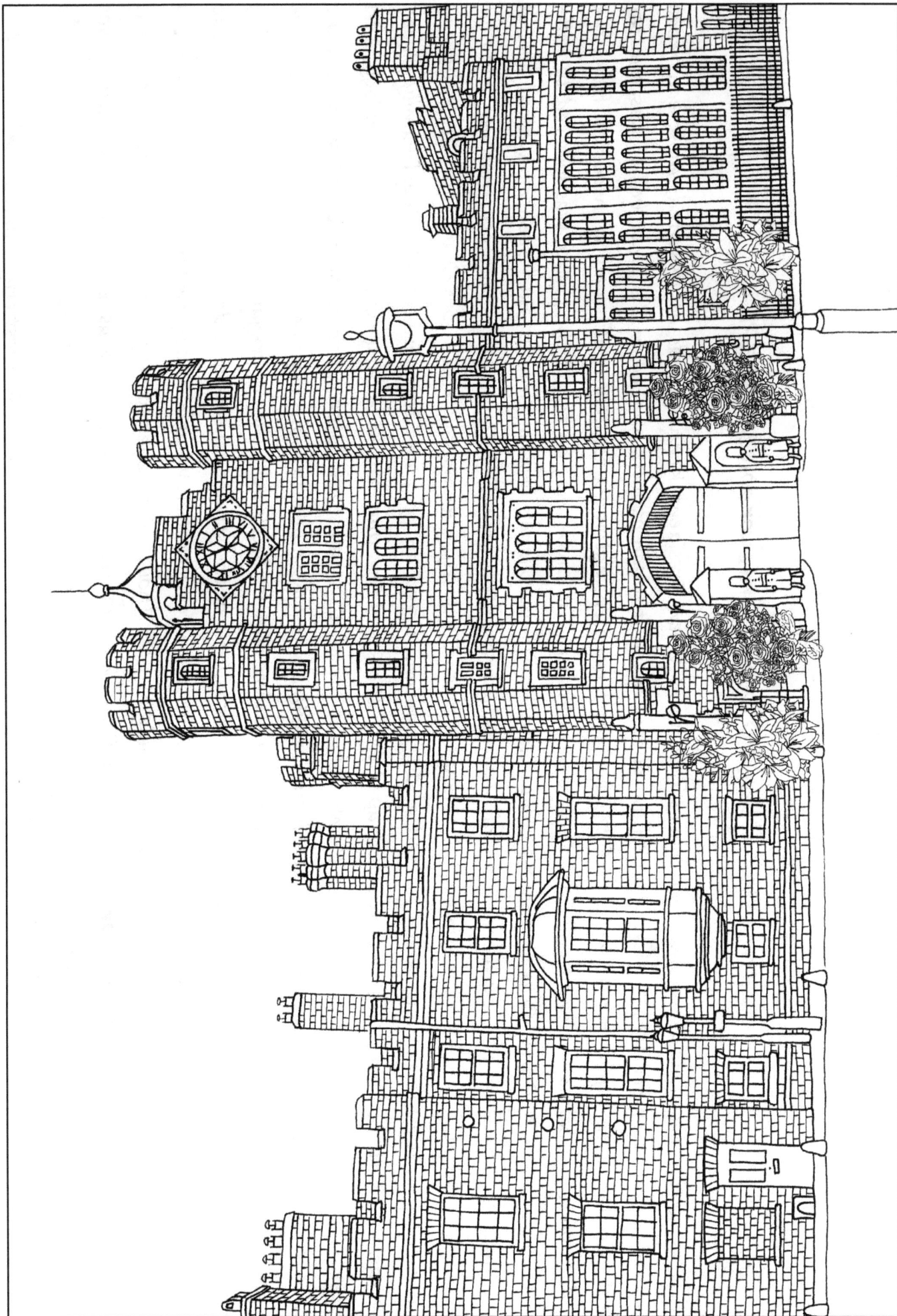

31

Westminster Abbey, 20 Deans Yard, London SW1P 3PA

Just as almost everyone can remember where they were when President Kennedy was assassinated, most can recall Saturday, 6 September 1997 when Diana's funeral took place. It began at 9.08 a.m. when the tenor bell of Westminster Abbey sounded to signal the departure of the cortege from Kensington Palace. The coffin was transported from the palace on a gun carriage along Hyde Park to St James Palace. The Union Flag on top of the palace was lowered to half-mast. Prince Philip, Prince Charles, Princes William and Harry and Diana's brother Charles, Earl Spencer, walked behind the funeral cortege on its way along The Mall. Two thousand people including Tony Blair, Margaret Thatcher, Sir Cliff Richard, Hillary Clinton, Henry Kissinger, Tom Cruise and Nicole Kidman attended the Abbey ceremony which started at 11 a.m. and lasted an hour and ten minutes. The Royal Family placed wreaths alongside Diana's coffin which was draped with the Royal Standard edged with ermine. In a moving eulogy, Earl Spencer, told the congregation, 'We give thanks for the life of a woman I am so proud to be able to call my sister, the unique, the complex, the extraordinary and irreplaceable Diana whose beauty, both internal and external, will never be extinguished from our minds.' As he finished speaking, waves of noise broke over the congregation – the sound of clapping from the thousands of people reverently listening to a broadcast of the service relayed outside the Abbey: 'It sounded like autumn leaves falling on a tin roof,' said Diana's Royal Protection Officer, Ken Wharfe. The hymns were 'I Vow to Thee, My Country', 'The King of Love My Shepherd Is' and 'Guide Me, Oh Thou Great Redeemer.' During the ceremony Elton John sang a revised version of his song 'Candle in the Wind' which now referred to the Princess as 'England's rose.' Diana was later laid to rest on a secluded island in the middle of a lake at her childhood home on the Althorp Estate.

This is the most tragic and senseless death –

Sir Elton John

32

10 Downing Street, SW1A 2AA

It was from the Prime Minister's office here on December 9, 1992 that John Major had drafted the announcement that Diana and Charles were to separate. In accordance with the Queen's wishes he said he wanted to make it clear that 'Their Royal Highnesses are not seeking a divorce' and he went on to say 'there was no reason why the Princess of Wales should not be crowned Queen in due course.' Nobody believed him but it took another three years for the formal announcement to be made. Diana said Major promised to make her an ambassador but never delivered.

From the same office on Monday 1 September 1997, Major's successor Tony Blair was to tell Bill Clinton in a telephone conversation in which they discussed Diana's death: 'It's like a star falling. The problem was the way she lived, in a Press frenzy. It's impossible to contemplate how intrusive it was, into every single aspect of her life. The last time I spoke with her, she said that were it not for her boys, she'd be off the board.' Mr. Clinton replied, 'Well I just feel so bad for her. She was just basically getting a hold of her life.' In a public statement Mr. Blair referred to Diana as 'the People's Princess.'

'I would like to represent this country abroad. Since I have all this media interest, let's not just sit and be battered by it, let's use it in a productive way to help this country.'

Diana on why she asked John Major if she could be an ambassador

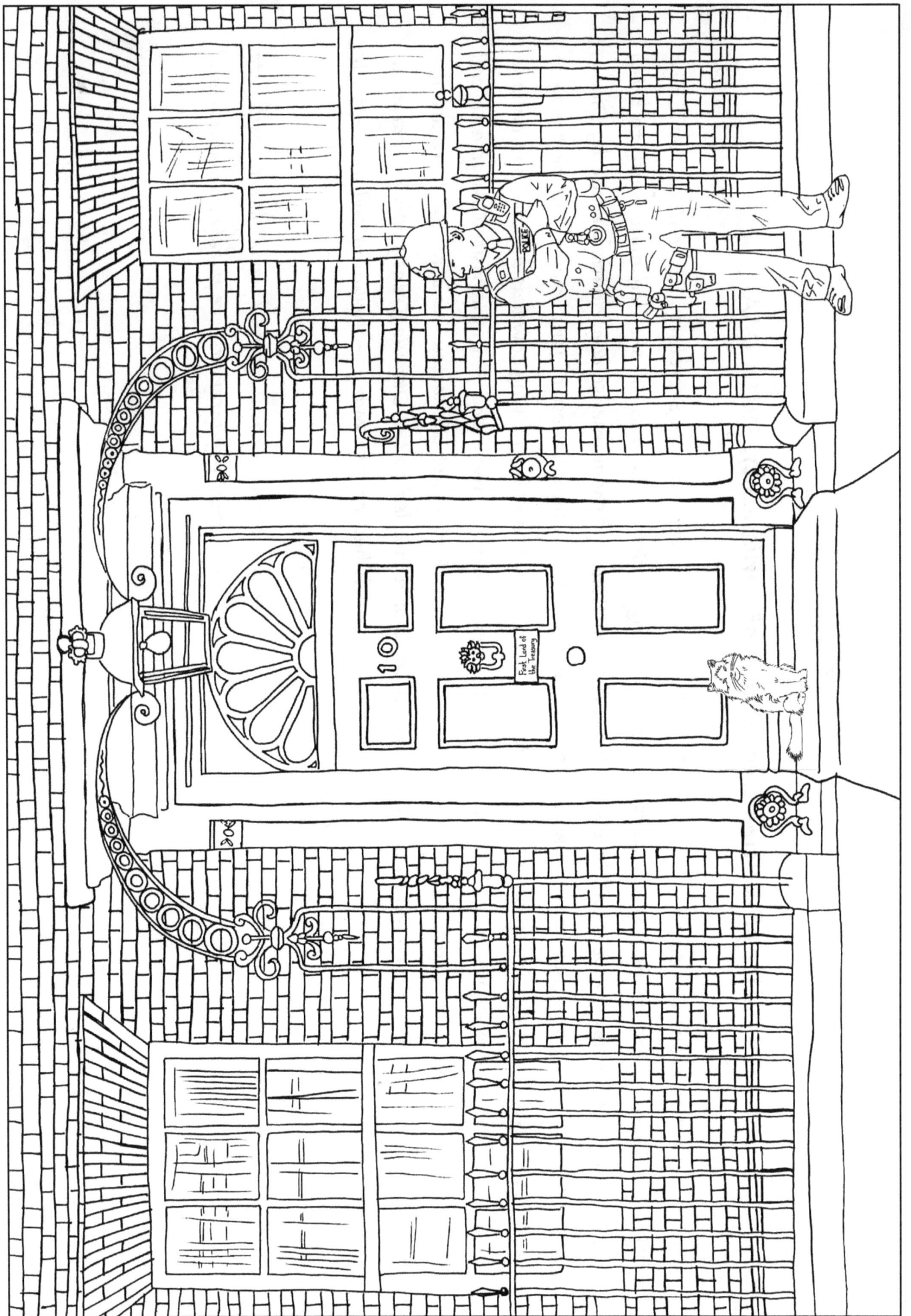

33

Palace of Westminster (Houses of Parliament), SW1A OAA

The House of Commons was silenced on July 10, 1998 when the-then Foreign Secretary, Robin Cook, 'paid high tribute to Diana's work as he introduced the Second Reading of the Landmines Bill she had done much to bring about: 'All Honourable Members will be aware from their postbags of the immense contribution made by Diana, Princess of Wales, to bringing home to many of our constituents the human cost of land mines. The best way in which to record our appreciation of her work is to pass the Bill and to pave the way towards a global ban on land mines,' he said. The previous year – just a few months before her untimely end – Diana visited Angola to call on landmine survivors in hospitals and tour de-mining projects. Pictures of Diana touring a minefield wearing a ballistic helmet and flak jacket were published around the world and led to the Ottawa Treaty which created an international ban on the use of anti-personnel landmines which had cost so many – including children – their lives and caused horrendous injuries to others.

'I am not a political figure. I would like to reiterate that my interests are purely humanitarian.'

Diana

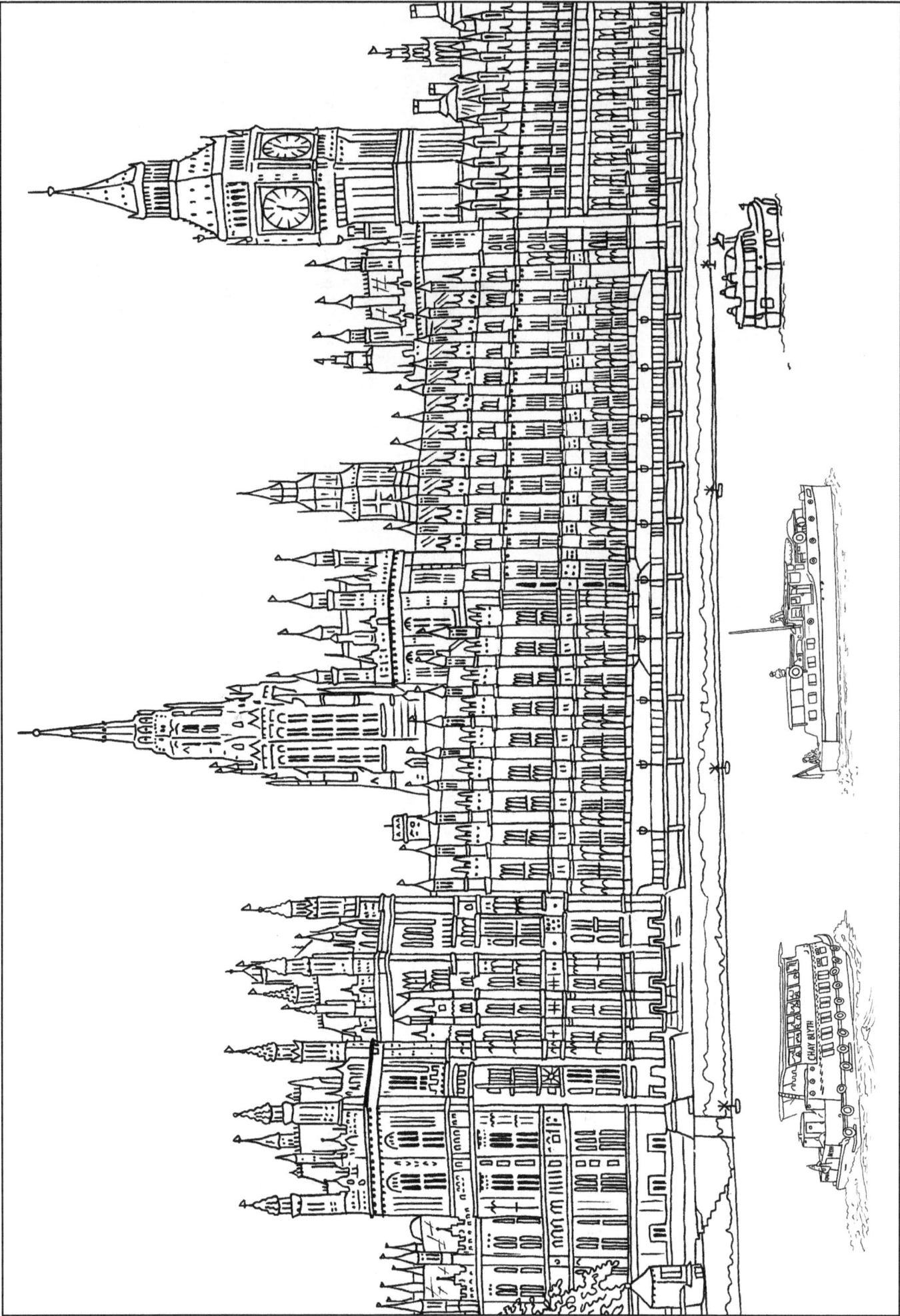

34

Diana Memorial Playground, Broad Walk, W2 4RU

It is fitting that this is one of the memorials to Diana who loved the innocence of childhood for this is truly a kiddies' wonderland. The centrepiece is an intricately detailed pirate ship moored aground in a sea of white sand. Children up to the age of twelve can clamber up the rigging all the way to the crow's nest, turn the giant wheel, explore the cabins and tug on a myriad of pulleys and ropes.

Beyond the land of pirates lies the teepee camp featuring a trio of wigwams, each large enough to hold a sizeable tribe of mini-Indians. Set against a lush background of scented shrubs, whispering willows, trees and bamboo, this royal Neverland is right here in the heart of London and is just the kind of place Diana would have taken William and Harry to when they were tots. There's even a cafe serving child platters. The Broad Walk runs between Black Lion Gate on Bayswater Road and Palace Gate on Kensington Road. The nearest underground station for the playground is Queensway.

'It's amazing how much happiness a small child brings to people.'

Diana

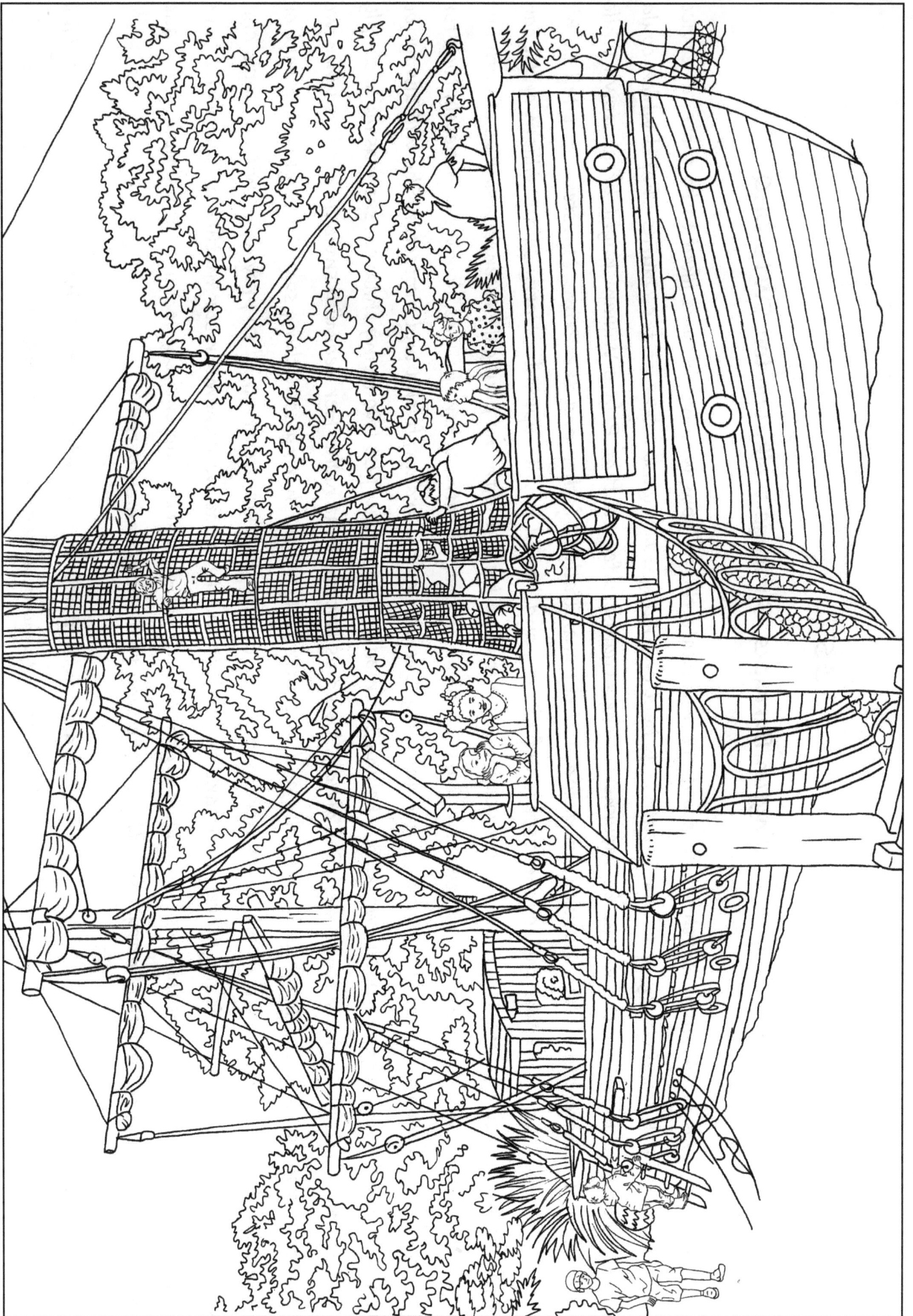

35

The Guards Chapel, Wellington Barracks, Birdcage Walk, London SW1E 6HQ

Because there was no venue on earth which could accommodate the millions who would have liked to be there, a service to mark the tenth anniversary of Diana's death was held on Friday 31 August 2007 at the Guards Chapel which could accommodate just 500 of the would-be mourners. The organisers feared that Prince William might break down while addressing a congregation that included his grandmother, grandfather, father and the Prime Minister, so it fell to his brother Prince Harry to make the toughest speech of his life, and he did it with aplomb. Harry said, 'William and I can separate life into two parts. There were those years when we were blessed with the physical presence beside us of both our mother and father. And then there are the ten years since our mother's death. When she was alive we completely took for granted her unrivalled love of life, laughter, fun and folly. She was our guardian, friend and protector. She will always be remembered for her amazing public work. But behind the media glare, to us, just two loving children, she was quite simply the best mum in the world. We miss her. She always kissed us last thing at night. Her beaming smile greeted us when we got home from school. She laughed hysterically and uncontrollably when sharing something silly she might have said or done that day. She encouraged us when we were nervous or unsure. She was determined to provide us with a stable and secure childhood. But what is far more important to William and I is that we remember our mother as she would have wished to be remembered, as she was – fun-loving, generous, down-to-earth, and entirely genuine. Put simply, she made us, and so many other people, happy. May this be the way that she is remembered.'

'You couldn't help but be entranced by Princess Diana . . . and I think everyone who met her fell in love with her a little, including myself.' –

Neil Diamond

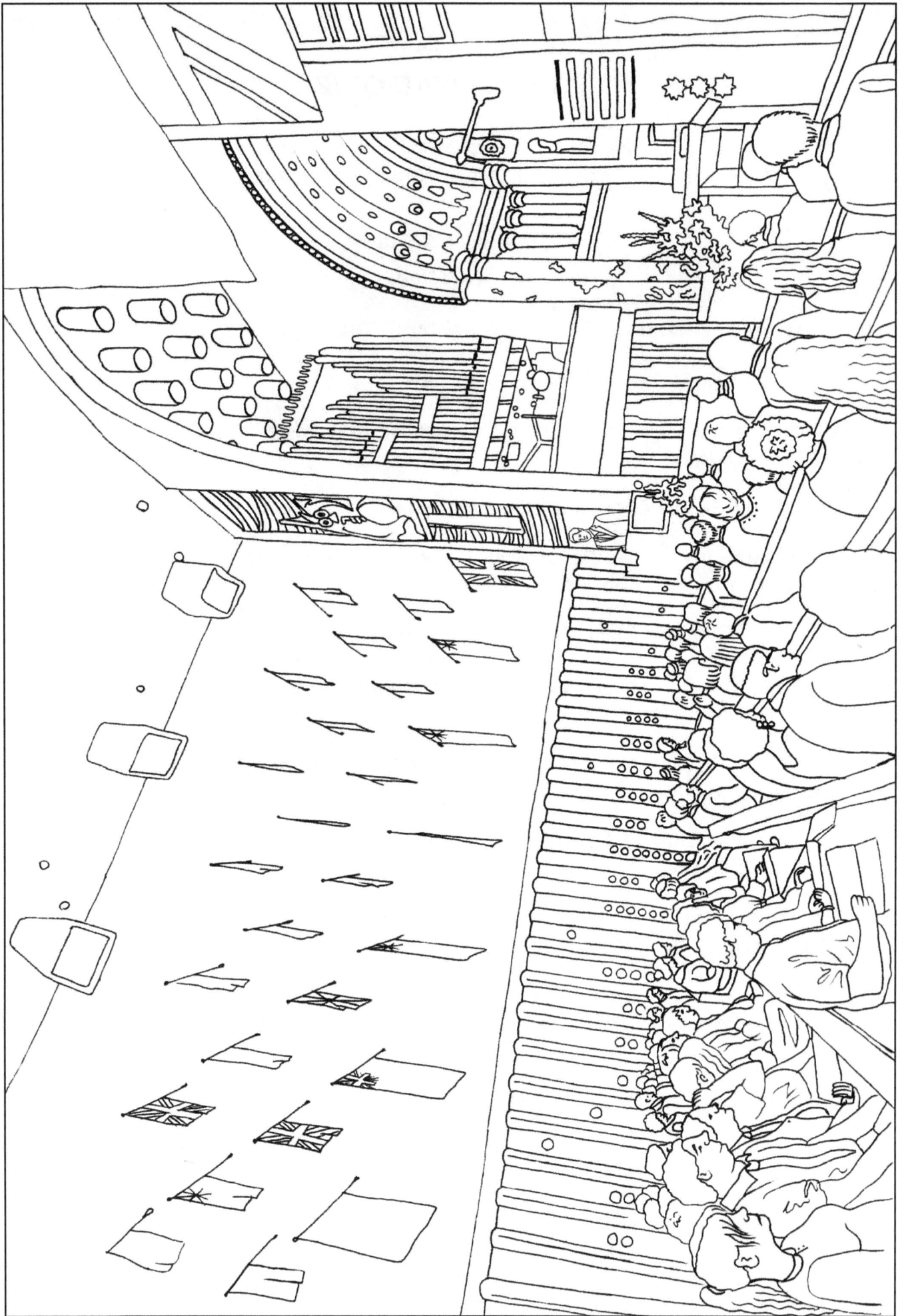

THE ROYAL QUIZ

This Diana quiz sorts the fans from the admirers – sure to be a favourite next Christmas in the Royal Salon bars

(Top score 25 points)

Questions

1. What are the names of Diana's two sisters? *Two points*

2. What was Diana's middle name? *One point*

3. What was the name of Diana's stepmother and what was Diana's nickname for her? *Two points*

4. Where did Prince Charles ask Diana to marry him? *One point*

5. Which member of the Royal Family served as one of Diana's bridesmaids at her wedding to Prince Charles on 29 July 1981? *One point*

6. Who made Diana's ivory silk taffeta wedding dress? *Two points*

7. Who was the hairdresser who did Diana's hair for the wedding and accompanied her on several overseas trips? *One point*

8. What was the name of the royal yacht in which Diana and Charles spent some of their honeymoon in 1981? *One point*

9. Which one of Diana's lovers called her 'Squidgy' and what name was given to the scandal of the Squidgy tape? *Two points*

10. At whose house did Diana confront Prince Charles and Camilla Parker Bowles about their affair? *One point*

11. Who conducted the BBC interview in which Diana said, 'Well, there were three of us in this marriage, so it was a bit crowded.' *One point*

12. Who was Diana referring to in the same interview when she said, 'Yes, I adored him. Yes, I was in love with him'? *One point*

13. Which aristocratic title did Diana share with Camilla Parker Bowles? *One point*

14. What was the name of the yacht in which Diana and Dodi Fayed enjoyed a Mediterranean holiday in August 1997? *One point*

15. Who was driving the Mercedes-Benz in which Diana and Dodi Fayed were killed in Paris on 31 August 1997? *One point*

36.
THE ROYAL QUIZ

16. What did Prime Minister Tony Blair call Diana in his statement to the nation in September 1997? *One point*

17. Who sang 'Candle in the Wind' at Diana's funeral and which two writers composed the song? *Two points*

18. What was the alternative title to 'Candle in the Wind 1997'? *One point*

19. Where is Diana buried? *One point*

20. Who gave the oration at the Guards Chapel, London, to commemorate the tenth anniversary of Diana's death in 2007? *One point*

THE ROYAL QUIZ

These are the answers

1. Sarah and Jane: Lady Elizabeth Sarah Lavinia McCorquodale (née Spencer and known as Sarah; born 19 March 1955) and Cynthia Jane Fellowes, Baroness Fellowes (née Spencer and known as Jane; born 11 February 1957). *Two points*

2. Frances, after her mother, the Honorable Frances Ruth Burke-Roche, daughter of the fourth Baron Fermoy, and later known as the Honorable Frances, Viscountess Althorp, and the Honorable Mrs Peter Shand Kydd. *One point*

3. Raine Spencer, daughter of novelist Dame Barbara Cartland and Alexander McCorquodale, though her mother later claimed that she was fathered by one of the sons of King George V, Prince George, the Duke of Kent. Diana called her 'Acid Raine'. *Two points*

4. In the nursery at Windsor Castle on 3 February 1981. *One point*

5. Lady Sarah Armstrong-Jones, seventeen-year-old daughter of the Earl of Snowdon and Princess Margaret. *One point*

6. David and Elizabeth Emanuel whose salon was in Brook Street, Mayfair, and later in Beauchamp Place, Knightsbridge. *Two points*

7. Kevin Shanley of the Head Lines salon in Thurlow Place, South Kensington. *One point*

8. Her Majesty's Yacht Britannia, more a luxury liner than a sailing boat. *One point*

9. James Gilbey, Old Etonian scion of the Gilbey gin-making family, who lived in Lennox Gardens, Chelsea, and whose astonishingly intimate conversation with Diana was recorded by a retired bank manager and published in The Sun as 'Squidgygate' on 23 August 1992. *Two points*

10. Lady Annabel Goldsmith's house at Ham Common, Richmond, Surrey. *One point*

11. Martin Bashir conducted the interview for the Panorama programme on 20 November 1995. *One point*

12. James Hewitt, the Cavalry officer who is often wrongly named as Prince Harry's real father. *One point*

13. Duchess of Cornwall. Duke of Cornwall is a non-hereditary peerage held by the Prince of Wales, the Sovereign's eldest son and heir, and at present no woman can be Duchess of Cornwall in her own right. *One point*

14. Jonikal. *One point*

THE ROYAL QUIZ

15. Henri Paul, who also died in the crash in the Pont d'Alma underpass. *One point*

16. The People's Princess. *One point*

17. Elton John performed 'Candle in the Wind' and Elton John and Bernie Taupin composed it. *Two points*

18. 'Goodbye England's Rose'. *One point*

19. Diana's grave is on an islet in an ornamental lake known as The Round Oval in the gardens of Althorp Park. *One point*

20. Prince Harry. *One point*

THE ROYAL QUIZ

Score:

25-20 points: The Royal Family themselves could not have done better

19-15 points: Clearly Diana interests you

14-10 points: You're getting there

Under 10 points: Need to read more!

By Chris Hutchins and Peter Thompson, authors of
the best seller *Diana's Nightmare: The Family*

Authors: CHRIS HUTCHINS AND
PETER THOMPSON

ABOUT THE BOOK Diana, Princess of Wales, died shortly before dawn on 31 August 1997 and yet she glows more visibly today than any other living royal or celebrity. Despite the passing of two decades, she remains the most iconic woman on the planet. Brave, beautiful, vulnerable and strong, she challenged the traditions of Buckingham Palace and, in death, not only changed the way we see the Royal Family but turned them into warmer, more self-aware, more accessible people. Even before Diana married into the most revered family on earth, she had her suspicions that the kith and kin of Prince Charles were not all they seemed. No sooner had she become the Princess of Wales and moved into Kensington Palace than her fears were confirmed: the House of Windsor constituted a flawed dynasty.

This compelling book reveals the secrets Diana discovered about her royal relatives. It reveals how angry and bitter the Queen was at her family's indiscretions; how the Queen Mother's indifference was matched only by Prince Philip's blind rage over Diana's determination to find her own path; what really went on between the Duke and Duchess of York; and how Prince Edward witnessed an unhappy Diana's tantrums at Balmoral.

It discloses how, one quiet Sunday afternoon at Highgrove, she discovered Charles's affair with Camilla Parker Bowles and how she confronted them about their duplicity in front of a witness at a society birthday party. Following the end of her marriage she was free to do whatever she wished. She enjoyed holidays with jet-set pals, found a soulmate who shared her humanitarian values, entertained whoever she wanted, and above all spent quality time with her boys, William and Harry, taking instruction from no one on how the young Princes should be raised. They would be the first to admit that Diana's real legacy – her legacy of love – belongs as much to the poor, the sick and the dispossessed of this world as it does to them.

This then is Diana's secret life. And much, much more . . . Parts of this book were included in an earlier edition - Diana' Nightmare: The Family.

Published by Neville Ness House
www.nevillenesshouse.com

HARRY
THE PEOPLE'S PRINCE

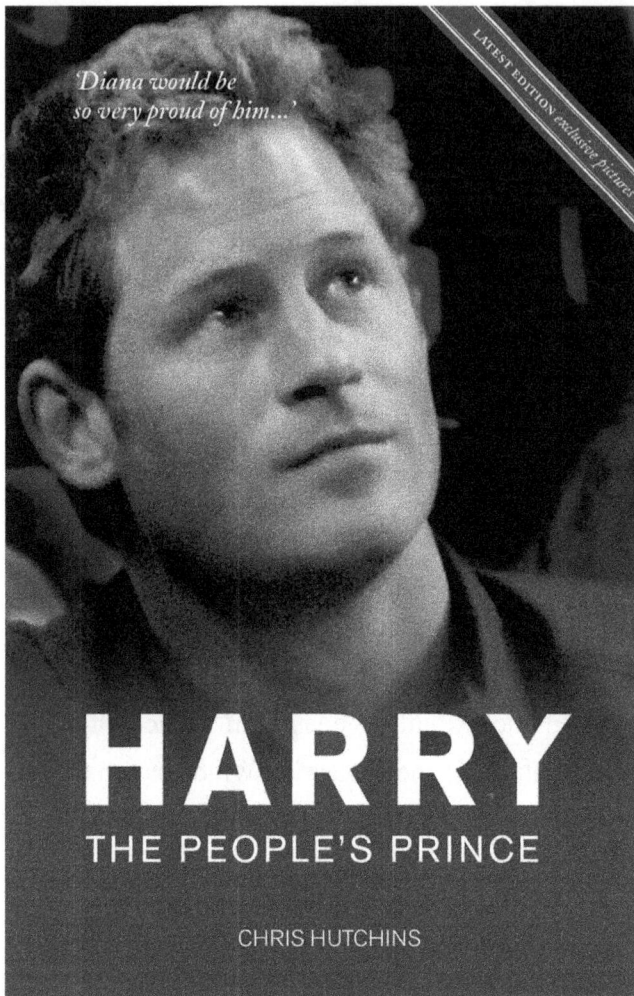

'Diana would be so very proud of him...'

LATEST EDITION exclusive pictures

HARRY
THE PEOPLE'S PRINCE
CHRIS HUTCHINS

Author CHRIS HUTCHINS

ABOUT THIS BOOK PRINCE HARRY is the most interesting – indeed the most exciting – member of the Royal Family and this no-holds-barred biography tells his story for the first time. Son of the late Princess Diana – the most famous woman on Earth – and Prince Charles, the next king, and brother of William, the king after that, he is determined to live by his mantra: 'I am what I am'.

From a childhood overshadowed by his parents' troubled marriage and scarred by the tragic death of his mother, to his brilliant public performances at the Queen's Diamond Jubilee celebrations, the London Olympics and his brother's wedding, this book charts the remarkable journey of a young man with an extraordinary destiny. Following in Diana's footsteps, his charitable works have taken him to far-flung corners of the world including Africa and the South Pole.

It also reveals details of his extraordinary love life, telling for the first time what caused his affair with Cressida Bonas to collapse.

The author has enjoyed unparalleled access to a wide variety of people whose lives Harry has touched: senior aides, humble members of palace staff, aristocrats, bodyguards, school friends, comrades-in-arms . . . and old flames. They piece together the tale of a young man who admirably has created a life so different from the one set out for him by what he describes as 'an accident of birth'

Published by Neville Ness House
www.nevillenesshouse.com

FERGIE CONFIDENTIAL
THE DUCHESS OF YORK'S TRUE STORY

Authors: CHRIS HUTCHINS AND
PETER THOMPSON

ABOUT THIS BOOK IT SEEMS that almost every week Sarah Ferguson - the Duchess of York, known to one and all as Fergie - makes headlines with her efforts to re-brand herself and explain her troubles. There are the weight-loss problems, the ongoing differences with the Royal Family and her financial difficulties. But how did it all start? It seemed like a fairy-tale come true when Sarah married the Queen's favourite son, Prince Andrew, and became one of the best-known women in the world. She was feted wherever she went – and she went everywhere. But the Duchess's world was to come crashing down in spectacular fashion.

We all heard the rumours, now here's a book that sets out the facts about all the scandals. Finally, the explosive truth from two experts – CHRIS HUTCHINS, the writer who broke the palace-rocking story of Fergie's risqué liaison with handsome Texan Steve Wyatt, and PETER THOMPSON, a former editor of London's Daily Mirror, the paper that ran the sexy St. Tropez stories of Fergie and her "financial advisor" Johnny Bryan. The book also details her often-tempestuous relationship with Princess Diana and how both women decided to end their marriages.

Published by Neville Ness House
www.nevillenesshouse.com

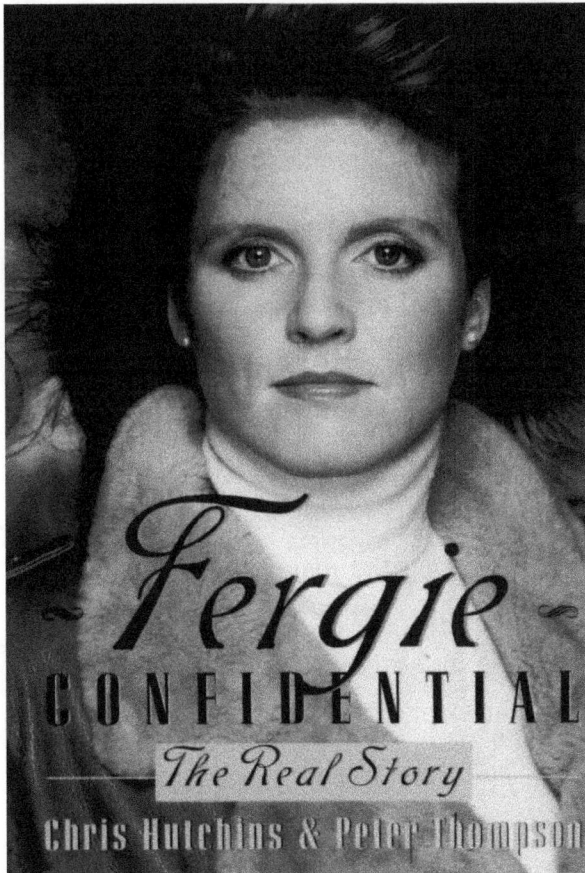

COLOURING IN THE MED

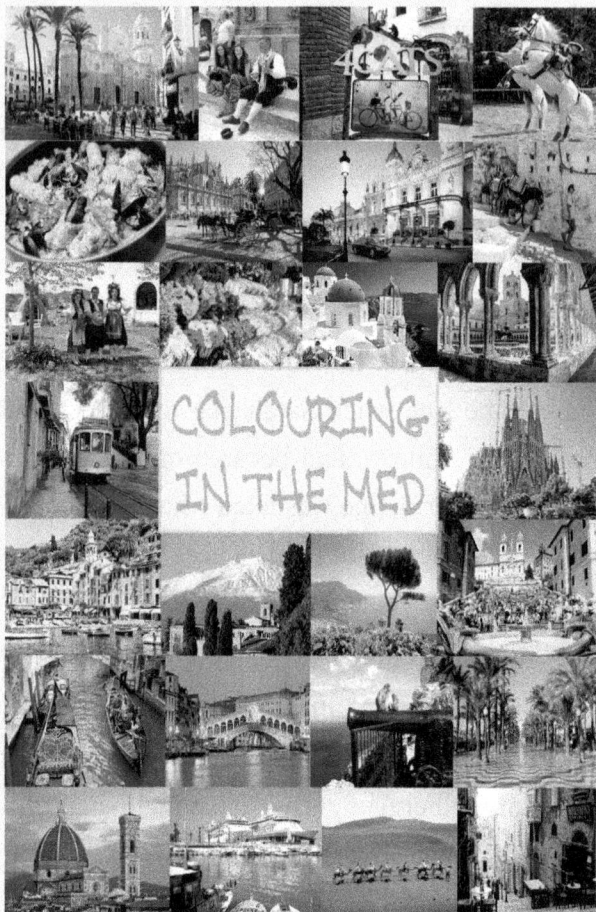

Illustrator/Author ANTONIO ROSSI AND
SARAH-JANE BENTLEY

Ever been on a journey through the golden cities that surround The Med? or Have you sat on the Spanish Steps in Rome? or could you imagine eating paella on the harbour at Portofino? or Ascended the steps to the top of the Leaning Tower of Pisa!

IT IS ALL POSSIBLE through this book of 50 illustrations and vignettes – **COLOURING IN THE MED.** A book that trail blazes you around the most amazing cities bringing the magic of The Med to life **MEMORIES or simply WISHES? COLOURING IN THE MED** will transport you and those close to you to make your dreams come true.

Fill your senses by colouring your way around the Med with these **50 illustrations of iconic scenes** you are likely to see or have seen on your travels. Accompanying each illustration is an interesting and entertaining vignette written by an award winning author. Make this a wonderful souvenir and visual diary full of happy memories either to share with family and friends or as a secret treasure trove of personal experiences embedded in the rivers of your memory forever. **It is a VISUAL DIARY, a WONDERFUL SOUVENIR**, drawing on the **GRAND TOURS**, and creating treasured memories of your journeys. Each book is available in two sizes, large (A4 - 8.5" x 11.0") or small (A5 - 5.5" x 8").

COLOURING IN THE MED engages you in an activity that nurtures mindfulness and mental agility. It promotes a fully engaged and agile mind.

Suitable for every generation, young and old. Indeed the activity can be an inter-generational shared experience between grandchildren and grandparents or mums and dads with their kids.

Paperback: 110 pages – Large (A4) and Small (A5), **Hardback** Large (A4)
Publisher: Neville Ness House; 1st edition (23 May 2017) www.nevillenesshouse.com
Language: English
ISBN-10: 0993445799/0957434588 /1999746902
ISBN-13: 978-0993445798/ 978-0957434585 /978-1999746902
Product Dimensions: 21.6 x 0.6 x 27.9 cm/ 13.3 x 0.6